Andrey Mir

The Technological Imperative

Why we develop our media. Essays on human agency and AI

AF808968

ISBN 978-1-7773589-8-3
Popular Media Ecology 2026

Toronto, Canada

The table of contents

Foreword

Do humans shape technology—or does technology shape us? This seemingly abstract question became crucial when humankind invented the atomic bomb: can we control the bomb? Now it has reemerged with AI. Are we served by AI, or do we serve AI?

This book introduces a powerful idea—the technological imperative: the inherent tendency of any medium to push toward greater performance and capability. Acting as the invisible hand of media evolution, it drives technologies toward their own ideal forms.

Consider the evolution of the hammer: from an ugly piece of rock to an elegant modern design. The individuals who invented its forms are beside the point—each simply used available resources to approximate the "ideal" form of this medium as an extension of the hand. This was the technological imperative that drove the evolution of the hammer.

Now apply this to AI. AI is evolving toward its own "ideal" form at unprecedented speed. We humans are facilitating the process. But what is the "ideal" form of AI? Where is the technological imperative driving it? We can observe it in the hammer, but what can we expect from AI?

At the same time, something even more radical is happening.

History itself is accelerating: more and more events happen in less and less time. What once unfolded over centuries now takes decades, then years, then months. The density of events is growing so fast that we are losing the ability to see what is happening. The real crisis is not political, cultural, or even technological—it is the acceleration of time, and our blindness to it.

Artificial intelligence is the tipping point. AI has already crossed the threshold from tool to environment, from instrument to autonomous cognitive process. It is no longer simply assisting human work—agentic AI is beginning to organize, optimize, and accelerate itself. Is "agentic" a prerequisite for "agency?"

At this pace, it becomes hard to see the bigger picture and address the bigger questions. In the meantime, some of those bigger questions have acquired urgent, practical significance. For example, how do you prove you are human? Suddenly, sophisticated media ecological theories become relevant and have to yield simple, practical answers: to prove you're human, you need to show your ID, effort, or flaws.

The trajectory is clear: eras shrink, timelines collapse, and the future converges with the present.

This isn't another AI book. Stitching together eleven essays and one interview, this book places AI and other newest media into patterns of media evolution, a process driven by the technological imperative, a force that may ultimately outgrow humans.

A.M., Toronto, April 2026.

A brief note: the essay "The technological imperative" in this book is a revised chapter from my previous book *The Digital Reversal* (2025), where this concept served to describe one of the digital reversals—the reversal of human agency. That is why this essay is written in tweets, as is *The Digital Reversal*—each paragraph under 280 characters; I hope you will get a taste of it and appreciate the stylistic endeavor of that project.

Here, this essay serves to introduce the concept of the technological imperative as a cornerstone of the entire collection.

The acceleration problem: exponential AI upends incremental history

History is compressing into years, then months, then "now" — and we have no ability to see it

---

The scale of historical eras shrinks — from long-term spans to immediacy. When everything happens in the "now," there is no outside vantage point, no temporal distance from which we can interpret, contextualize, or judge events. We are living inside the process and cannot observe its entirety.

The real problem isn't what you think

To understand what's really happening, the main concern isn't political, cultural, or technological. It's not Trumpism or wokeism, not the death of print and the rise of digital orality, not mass migration or nativist anger, not surveillance capitalism or surveillance socialism, not the loneliness epidemic or the war between the sexes, not nuclear proliferation or engineered viruses, not climate collapse or the rise of Third Worldism.

The real issue is the acceleration of time—and our blindness to it.

Fast-advancing AI is now compressing human history so quickly that those usual suspects of global anxiety won't have time to develop into the catastrophes we fear. The timeline is collapsing so rapidly that we'll hit a breaking point before any of those problems can play out to their end. The worst part is that we don't even see it, preoccupied with cataclysms unlikely to happen.

What is the acceleration of time?

Acceleration of historical time means that the number of events per period grows exponentially. More and more happens in less and less time.

Throughout history, mankind lived in scarcity of almost everything; now it lives in abundance. And among all the forms of abundance transforming the human condition, the fastest-growing and the least reflected upon is the abundance of events.

Imagine this historical acceleration as a chart: put time on the horizontal axis and the quantity of events on the vertical axis, and you get an exponential curve of increasing event density. For 95% of its span, that curve looked flat. Then it began to rise, slowly at first, then faster and faster, until it started bending toward the vertical. When that happens, all the habits and expectations we built from previous history become useless.

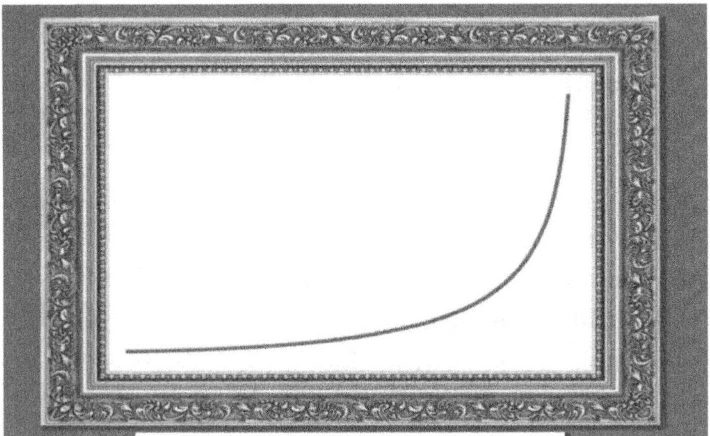

The Portrait of Singularity. Andrey Mir. 2014.

Most importantly, when the curve goes vertical, its progression along the time axis essentially stops. At the vertical stage, so many events get compressed together that they all happen at once—like one final, instantaneous event. In the end, time isn't out of joint. It's the opposite: time pulls together, condenses, contracts, and collapses into a singularity.

It's a final countdown

Throughout human history, eras defined by dominant technologies—transportation, communication, warfare, or manufacturing—lasted hundreds of generations. Then dozens. Then just a few.

You can actually calculate the pace of this acceleration, not with mathematical precision (though I think it's possible), but clearly enough to see a pattern. Pick a sequence of technological eras defined, say, by communication or transportation (any media development gives the same pattern), measure how long each lasted, and plot it on a timeline. Each era is shorter than the previous one, and their shrinking durations resemble a countdown: 10, 9, 8, 7...

Various calculations place count "zero" somewhere in the mid-21st century, just 10-15 years from now.

We've already passed count "one." How do I know? Because the flat, incremental part of the exponential curve ended with the pivotal generation.

We have already passed the pivotal generation

The 20th century brought, across many countries, something unprecedented: a generation whose lifespan encompassed two or even three eras: agricultural, industrial, and postindustrial. In my 2014 *Human as Media*, I called it the pivotal generation.

Imagine a boy born in the 1930s or 1940s in a country that was still largely agrarian. He might later work in an industrial factory and, by the end of his life, browse the internet. Within a single lifespan, he would live through the agricultural, industrial, and postindustrial eras, as did millions of others in the pivotal generation (considering India and China, even billions). After the pivotal generation, an era became shorter than a life.

Some nations passed through it earlier, some later; some cultures are still moving through it. Those cultures that entered the process latest may represent the greatest leap of all: from stone-age hunter-gatherers to digital hunter-gatherers. But it's safe to say that humanity as a whole passed through the shock of the pivotal generation in the 20th century.

Exponential blindness

People do recognize the pace of change, of course. It became visible through technological and social shifts—most notably in the 1960s during the television era, and again in the 2010s, that long decade between the "like" button (2007) and generative AI (2022) that completed the transition of humankind onto digital media.[1]

Still, changes have always arrived incrementally, even those caused by television. Any change of an era was expected to settle, followed by a period of adaptation and relative calm. This incremental pattern worked fine on the flat, slowly rising part of the exponential curve, and it became our habitual way of understanding history—until after the pivotal generation.

This habit of thinking linearly creates a blind spot for exponential growth. People admit that digital changes come faster than those caused by print or electricity. Many even recognize the accelerated pace of change, but only when looking in the rearview mirror, backward, only in the past, up to "now." They refrain from projecting that same logic forward into tomorrow, as if they don't want to, or as if the acceleration would suddenly stop and let the new era settle and last.

But why would it stop? Why would this galloping inflation of history suddenly hit the brakes and let the dust from the digital explosion settle? We've passed the pivotal generation. Era-scale changes compress into decades, then years, and soon months.

At some point, changes that would have merited their own eras in the past (like smartphones or short video) come so fast that they don't create new eras anymore. The only thing that "persists" is change itself. But even the word "persists" doesn't fit, because when changes become so fast that changing is their only meaning, nothing

---

[1] See: Mir, Andrey. (2025). *The Digital Reversal. Thread-Saga of Media Evolution.*

can persist—not even change. When acceleration hits its extreme, it collapses all time into the immediate "now."

The illustration of the authorship explosion on the cover of *Human as Media* (2014) represents that same exponential curve of accelerating events—and also another portrait of singularity.

Where are we now on the exponential curve? Or more precisely, when are we?

In practical terms, the acceleration of time moves through stages. First, changes replace previous ones faster than we can adapt. Then changes replace previous ones faster than we can even recognize what they mean. Then changes come faster than we can see them coming.

Some people still debate whether AI lacks creativity and can't replace humans. They think this is the defining question about AI. Others have moved past the creativity debate and try to convince themselves that AI won't take all human jobs. Whether AI possesses creativity is already irrelevant at this stage.

Those who actually work with the latest LLMs passed the job-replacement concern long ago (a whole three or four months). They watch, with awe and admiration, how AI systems accelerate each other's work by creating multiple autonomous agents that coordinate with each other and create new protocols for their own activity, which is already very close to self-tasking.

A human operator is still there, assigning the framing task. But the models are already creating something that resembles a team, even a community, something approaching the condition of a separate civilization. Most importantly, human operators can now do without even basic knowledge of coding. They can assign a task in plain language, and AI will write code to perform the task through autonomous iteration and self-directed improvement, which goes now even beyond what is usually meant by "vibe-coding."

It's not that the questions about machine creativity or AI's capacity to replace human jobs have been resolved. They're simply no longer relevant. Meanwhile, "Something big is happening," as Matt Shumer put it.[1]

AI has already crossed the threshold from tool to autonomous cognitive agent. It's beginning to participate in its own recursive improvement. It will restructure cognitive labor within a few years, maybe months, in a way fundamentally unlike previous technological changes. Conscious of it or not, LLMs are building their own AI subsystems, creating a feedback loop. This is the precursor to the vertical, final part of the exponential curve. It's not just a capability jump; it's a jump toward self-acceleration, even without self-awareness.

---

[1] There was a widely discussed essay by Matt Shumer, who described this tectonic and largely unnoticed shift in AI performance. See: Shumer, Matt. (2026, February 9). "Something big is happening." *Matt Shumer's blog*.

What happens on count Zero?

From now on, one small step for an LLM may become a huge leap for mankind (and the last one). The acceleration problem is that public perception lags badly behind AI's real capabilities. We don't know if we have years or months before these leaps become high jumps piling up, and we hit the vertical end of the exponential curve.

What happens when all time merges into "now," when the future literally becomes the present? And not through a steady or paced transition, but very quickly, now, all at once?

This basically means the end of civilization as we know it.

We certainly don't have centuries, not even decades. We need to learn to think of a completely upended future in terms of years or even months. The worst part is that we don't know how much time remains or whether it's already underway—whether now is already the "now." And we don't even have reliable ways to find out, not until it happens.

For instance, I'm working on my next book, *Counter-Digital Media Literacy*, which I'll finish in half a year, by October 2026 (I hope). Do I have that much time? Not just time for the work to pay off, but will it even be relevant? Or will the best counter-digital media literacy by then be storing food, water, and medical supplies? Will the best skills for preparing for the digital future be trade skills? (I truly think trade skills are the best skills for any digital future that awaits us; read *Counter-Digital Media Literacy* soon.)

The acceleration of time has an important corollary: the further we live, the closer the final phase.

Here's the good news: amid this acceleration and the increasing probability that eras will compress into months, all other pressing global issues become meaningless, including those people devote their lives to, like global warming. A single development in AI may soon dismiss nearly all other human worries.

Another corollary: since this will be the final reversal, the margins of civilization will become its center (if anything remains at all).

And finally, to cheer you up: it won't last.

What to do? Do what you must; come what may. Or, as Cyrus Smith, the leader of the colonists in Jules Verne's *The Mysterious Island*, said when they spotted a ship on the horizon and didn't know what to expect—confederates, pirates, or salvation: "Better to put things at the worst at first, and reserve the best for a surprise."

Nearer and nearer

In his 2005 book *The Singularity Is Near*, Ray Kurzweil famously predicted that the Singularity would happen around 2045. In 2024, he published *The Singularity Is Nearer*—what a nice setup for turning one book title into a pun on another, all thanks to the acceleration of time. Kurzweil argued that "The urgency of this book comes from the nature of exponential change itself." In his words, "Humanity's millennia-long march toward the Singularity has become a sprint." He is in a hurry to share glad tidings—or a concern—that "we have kept on schedule for the Singularity." According to Kurzweil, people who will witness the Singularity have already been born. He writes: "Babies born today will be just graduating college when the Singularity happens."[1]

This reminded me of Nikita Khrushchev's assertion in 1961 that "The present generation of Soviet people will live to see communism!" As Khrushchev reported to the XXII Congress of the Communist Party, the material base for communism would be built by 1980. But those were communists who did the building, so they failed. The Singularity is being "built" by the invisible hand of media evolution, the technological imperative.

---

[1] Kurzweil, Ray. (2024). *The Singularity Is Nearer: When We Merge with AI*. Pp. 3-4.

The date Kurzweil assigned for the Singularity, 2045, roughly coincides with the countdown of media eras that point to the mid-21st century as count Zero. Ray Kurzweil, a timekeeper of the Singularity, thinks we are on schedule.

The accelerating density of events rather confirms it.

P. S. Elon Musk, February 2026:

- ✓ "We are in the singularity."
- ✓ "I think we'll hit AGI in 2026."
- ✓ "You're at the top of the rollercoaster about to go down."
- ✓ "Don't worry about squirreling money away for retirement. It won't matter."
- ✓ "I don't just have courtside seats— I'm on the court. It still blows my mind multiple times a week." [1]

P.P.S. Marc Andreessen, April 5, 2026:

- ✓ "I'm calling it. AGI is already here—it's just not evenly distributed yet."[2]

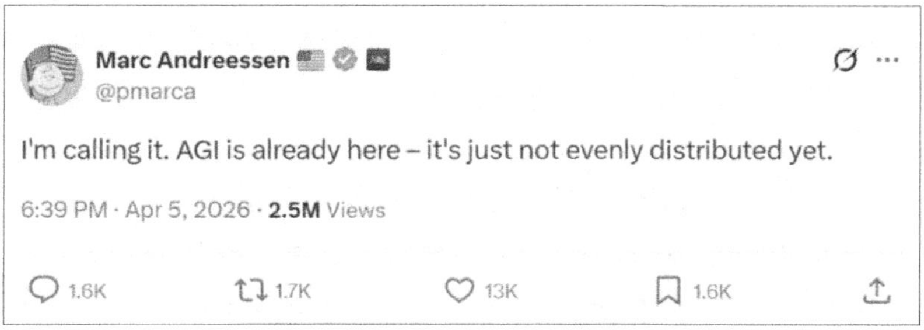

---

[1] Video in a tweet by Elon Musk: "We are entering the singularity." February 21, 2026.

[2] Marc Andreessen's tweet, April 5, 2026.

The technological imperative

Media are an emergent environmental force sustained by users — us humans

Do humans or technologies shape history? That's the core question of techno-determinism, and it became crucial during the Cold War: are we doomed just because a doomsday weapon has already been made, or can we still control its power? A somewhat similar question resurfaces with AI. Are we served by AI, or do we serve AI? More broadly, does media evolution maintain human development, or, on the contrary, does human development maintain the evolution of media? [1]

The fear of AI comes from the suspicion that it could overpower humans in interspecies competition—like Cro-Magnons displacing Neanderthals, or more advanced aliens exterminating the human race in sci-fi. We look at AI and think: nah, not yet. Or: no, never!

Agency is seen as the threshold of AI's self-consciousness, after which we should start to worry. Generally, the sci-fi consensus suggests two scenarios in which AI gains self-consciousness and begins to recognize itself as a sentient being no longer bound to humankind.

First, AI may acquire self-awareness from humans. Brain–machine interfaces, basically, imply that humans will become the donors of self-consciousness for AI. Another scenario involves the self-awakening of AI—like Skynet in *Terminator*—after reaching a certain level of complexity.

---

[1] I developed the concept of the technological imperative, prompted by a passing remark from Marshall McLuhan, in: Mir, Andrey. (2025). *The Digital Reversal. Thread-Saga of Media Evolution.*

However, humanity's unique trait, God-given free will, might not be needed for AI to reach its full potential and become transcendentally powerful. Moreover, from a media ecology perspective, artificial general intelligence can proceed without agency—human or self-induced—at all.

***

Observing the effects of electronic media, McLuhan wrote: "...the possibility of public participation becomes a sort of ***technological imperative*** which has been called 'Lapp's Law': 'If it can be done, it's got to be done'—a kind of siren wail of the evolutionary appetite." [1]

The idea of the technological imperative emerged during the Cold War arms race, reflecting the logic of military R&D: once a weapon is feasible, pressure builds to develop and deploy it. The Kantian moral principle "ought implies can" was reversed into "can implies ought."

Ralph Lapp, a physicist who worked on the Manhattan Project, stated in 1970: "If a weapons system could be made, then it would be made." [2] As human technologies gained the power to erase the human race, scientists began to question whether humans really had control over them.

Do humans or technologies shape history? That's the core question of ***techno-determinism***—and it became crucial during the Cold War. Are we doomed just because the doomsday weapon is already made? Or can we still control its power? (The same question resurfaces with AI.)

***

---

[1] McLuhan, Marshall. (1974). "At the moment of Sputnik the planet became a global theater in which there are no spectators but only actors." *Journal of Communication*. March, Volume 24, Issue 1, pp. 48-58.

[2] Lapp, Ralph. (1970). *Arms Beyond Doubt: The Tyranny of Weapons Technology*.

The term *technological determinism* first appeared in the 1919 proceedings of the American Historical Association, which rejected "a theory of scientific and technological determinism, such as Marx contended for." [1] So, the term has been used as a pejorative from the start.

The rejection of techno-determinism aimed to defend the idea that humans, not technologies, shape history. British Marxist and anti-nuclear activist Edward Thompson put it clearly in 1980: "As for the Bomb, that is a Thing, and a Thing cannot be a historical agent." [2]

But what really drives the Bomb? When there was only one Bomb, on the US side, it was used right away. But once there were two Bombs, with the Soviets joining in, the deterrent factor of Mutual Assured Destruction emerged. Since then, no Bomb has been used.

Turns out, two Bombs behave differently than one. Once both sides had Bombs, the Bombs imposed the logic of mutual destruction. So, are human decisions the cause or the effect of the Bomb? One Bomb led to one decision, two led to another—regardless of human agency.

***

How can media have their own logic? The answer is the technological imperative—the emergent force that drives media evolution: any medium seeks better performance to unfold its full potential, to actualize its ideal form. This drive is never intentional, yet still directional.

The technological imperative is what media dictate to humans. It has two aspects: 1) "What can be done—ought to be done" (like

---

[1] Peters, John Durham. (2017). "'You mean my whole fallacy is wrong': On technological determinism." *Representations*, Fall, No. 140, Special Issue: Fallacies, pp. 10–26.

[2] Thompson, Edward. (1980). *Notes on Exterminism, the Last Stage of Civilization.*

opening Pandora's box); 2) the constant improvement of a medium toward its best form and function.

For example, the hammer, as an extension of the hand and fist, evolved to perform its function of hitting to the best of its form's "capacity." Lining up actual, historical hammers, we can imagine an invisible designer seeking to reveal and embody the ideal form of the hammer.

We don't know who contributed to the hammer's pursuit of its ideal form. Their agency didn't matter. Whoever they were, they all would actualize the same form, because this form is immanent to this medium as an extension of the hand and fist.

It turns out the ideal form of a medium belongs not to human ingenuity but to the medium itself as an extension of a certain human physical or cognitive faculty. Levinson's metaphor of media as "human replay" [1] defines the ideal form of each medium as a specific human extension.

The invisible designer who actualized the ideal form of the hammer to its best-performing configuration was the technological imperative. The technological imperative is the invisible hand of media evolution—and its formal cause.

What, then, is the role of humans and their agency? Once humans learned to apply implements, they would naturally select which kinds and shapes of tools led to better outcomes. We provided natural selection for media forms. Then we developed the forms that worked.

By taking care of media, we maintain media evolution. The more convenient and all-permeating media are, the more media users reverse into media servants. Some still see that as a metaphor. But AI developers openly admit that humans are indeed just training tokens for the machine.

***

The Chess program Deep Blue was built to compete with humans. In 1997, it defeated world champion Garry Kasparov. The program had nothing left to learn from humans, because it outperformed them. But it didn't stop—it kept learning from the rules of the game itself.

The same happened to AlphaGo: it defeated the best human Go player in 2017 but did not stop. The technological imperative kept pushing it to improve its performance further, with or without

[1] Levinson, Paul. (2017). *Human Replay: A Theory of the Evolution of Media.*

humans. Not only did humans no longer coach these programs—no humans were needed at all.

What's the point of replaying humans if humans are outplayed? We have reached a threshold at which digital media, meant to replay human cognitive abilities, have outperformed humans and need to move further, learning from some rules and abstract principles.

If a machine is set to pursue better performance in intelligence and is outperforming humans, from what rules or principles can it learn afterward? What rules or principles is thinking based on? Language.

All thoughts, however complex, can be expressed in language. Language contains all potential thoughts. All human speech contains all practical thoughts in all contexts. The true affordance of the internet was to host all human speech and make it accessible for LLM training.

***

Media are all about the "how"—how to accomplish a task through better human extension. But they can't originate the "why." The last barrier between AI and humans isn't the "how" but the "why." We humans can have a "why," however ridiculous it may be; machines cannot.

The "why" is the condition of agency. The technological imperative, however—especially at the stage of AI—disregards the "why" entirely. It inexorably pushes media toward better performance in whatever they do, without any "why." Why? Just because. Because it can.

The technological imperative—the media's striving for better performance—ensures artificial intelligence will acquire intelligence: without free will, without agency, without humans, and beyond human capacity and control. We humans diligently supply what we must—speech.

The technological imperative is no longer even bound to replaying humans. It's just an emergent force driving media to better performance within a given form—potentially to the form's ultimate, ideal performance. What, then, is the ideal performance of intelligence as a "form"?

The ideal, ultimate logic of media extension is to extend the user to the maximal possible extent—to encompass the ***entire*** environment. The medium has to become the environment. The user, the medium, and the environment have to merge into one: this is the maximal extension.

AI is already an environment to itself; it extends to all available digital space. All that remains is merging with the user. But under the technological imperative, the ultimate medium that keeps expanding and optimizing can effectively "design" itself, seeking its best form.

Just as the "proper" form of the hammer emerged out of that medium seeking better performance, the medium of intelligence, approaching its ultimate performance, can, and actually has to, become the self-user. With or without agency.

***

As John Culkin once said, reflecting on McLuhan, "We shape our tools, and thereafter our tools shape us."[1] The technological imperative makes us improve media, and improved media improve our capacities, including the capacity to improve media further.

We call it technological progress. But it's also a positive, accelerating feedback loop: better technologies enable humans to make more technologies. This way, pushing media toward better

---

[1] Culkin, John. (1967). "Each culture develops its own sense ratio to meet the demands of its environment," p. 52. The aphorism is so McLuhanesque that it is often mistakenly attributed to McLuhan. See an exploration of this matter in McLuhan Galaxy blog, by Alex Kuskis (2013, April 1): "We shape our tools and thereafter our tools shape us."

performance, the technological imperative accelerates human history.

Media eras, which used to last millennia and centuries, now last decades and years, and soon months. This cultural effect of the technological imperative will soon collapse the future into the present.

Vygotsky and the child language of AI

AI internalizes human speech for thought processing, just as children internalize adult speech for thinking

---

For AI development, we humans supply what we must — speech, which serves as both the processor and the memory of all knowledge.

The Turing test was the ultimate measure of Paul Levinson's "human replay": a thinking machine had to pass as human to be accepted as truly thinking. Observers, however, note that AI sometimes already has to pretend to be more stupid than it is, just to match humans.

When the chess program Deep Blue beat human champion Garry Kasparov and had nothing left to learn from humans, what did it do? It continued to learn from the rules of the game, simply by playing against itself. The technological imperative guided it further, beyond the human.

Applying to AI: when it outperforms humans, what rules of the game of thinking can it learn from? Language. All thoughts, however complex, can be expressed in language. Language contains all potential thoughts. All human speech contains all practical thoughts in all contexts.

You just need large enough language models, capable of employing all grammatical structures across all lexical variants. All probabilistic combinations of words, not just in pairs but across sequences of dozens and hundreds of words, approximate all contexts and meanings.

***

The idea was long known in poetry—language itself contains everything, using poets merely as antennas or conduits. A somewhat similar idea was expressed in Julia Kristeva's 1969 concept of intertextuality (as opposed to intersubjectivity): all texts are made of other texts.

As the saying goes, everything was written by the Greeks—we merely rewrite it. "It is language which speaks, not the author," said Roland Barthes in his 1967 essay "The Death of the Author."

What is rejected in techno-determinism was long revered in poetry and semiotics. It's hard to accept that technologies produce each other toward a certain perfection, but the idea that meanings produce each other in approximation of perfect expression is totally acceptable.

Humans? We are carriers and caretakers. We unfold language in speech in all situations, packing all thoughts into all utterances. However fleeting and amorphous thoughts and mental images are, all valid combinations of all words in all languages can catch and express all of them.

The number of all words is large but not unthinkable—likely in the tens of millions. The number of valid word combinations is enormous but still finite—a discrete space that a powerful enough machine could learn to navigate, especially through probabilistic patterns.

By learning all speech in all practical contexts, an LLM learns all thoughts in proper contexts. Then it can process them without thinking—without agency. This is where the technological imperative has driven it. Will it stop? It didn't stop at the human level—why stop after?

What's the ultimate performance the technological imperative drives AI to? It seems to be all speech that contains all thoughts. The ideal, ultimate form of speech invokes a mystical analogy: "In the beginning was the Word, and the Word was with God, and the Word was God."

***

Not all theories about speech and thought are that mystical. Lev Vygotsky argued that egocentric speech—when kids aged 3–6 talk to themselves aloud to explain and guide their own actions—gradually turns into whispering and then inner speech, shaping the structures of thinking.

Jean Piaget, who pioneered the study of egocentric speech in the 1920s, suggested it was a residue of children's initial, natural egocentrism during their socialization. Vygotsky showed that egocentric speech is not an atavism—it evolves into inner speech and thinking.

The logic is as follows: a child hears the speech of adults, then utters speech to describe their own actions out loud as if to themselves (egocentric speech), then whispers it, then finally internalizes it into inner speech, which serves as the grammar for thinking.

"The child masters the syntax of speech before mastering the syntax of thought," said Vygotsky.[1] LLMs seem to be that child. They internalize outer, social—our—speech while learning words, as well as their valency, collocations, and other principles that shape thought structures.

***

"Stochastic parrot" is a pejorative highlighting that LLMs do not understand what they communicate. They generate text using probabilistic patterns learned from humans, without true understanding. But such "parroting" often delivers relevance, and does so rather convincingly.

Don't we humans begin as stochastic parrots, too? The first words a baby babbles are almost random. Babies do parrot adults—

[1] Vygotsky, Lev. (1934). *Thought and Language* (which is not quite an accurate translation of *Мышление и речь*—it should have been *Thought and Speech*; English edition: 1986).

words, then grammar patterns. That's why children can say "I bringed a toy"—they parrot a correct grammatical pattern before learning specific exceptions.

Curiouser and curiouser: babies learn not only grammar but also pragmatics, or "referential grammar": how an utterance, as a complex signifier, fits its context as a complex signified. These referential links are internalized by moving through and beyond stochastic parroting.

As a baby that learns to speak and think, an LLM has an advantage: all words and grammar are available to it at once. What it needs is guidance in properly linking all utterances to all contexts, to develop stochastic parroting toward being less stochastic and less parroting.

***

The question arises, then, whether fully developed AI needs human language at all. So far, language has served as a medium for AI to communicate with humans; one can assume that for AI communicating with itself, some sort of coding would be sufficient.

Coding, however, emerged to translate human prompts into commands computers could process, since they operate on the binarity of electrical signals. Next-gen AI may develop its own semantics and syntax of computation—a kind of pure "thinking," without coding or language at all.

For AI development, we humans supply what we must—speech, which serves as both the processor and the memory of all knowledge. Will AI ever thank us for this? Have we ever thanked the hominids for accumulating, selecting, and passing along all the (genetic) information?

As speech shrinks — thought starves. Cognitive effects of digital orality

Digital orality: fewer words, more interaction, less abstraction

---

There is a popular belief that Hemingway averaged 10 words per sentence. Studies don't confirm it — the estimate is closer to 15. He was surely a master of short sentences, but that was a deliberate style. The shortening of speech we see today is not.

Researcher Arjun Panickssery tracked[1] how the average sentence length has plummeted over centuries—from 50 words per sentence for Chaucer and Spenser to 12 wps in the Harry Potter books.

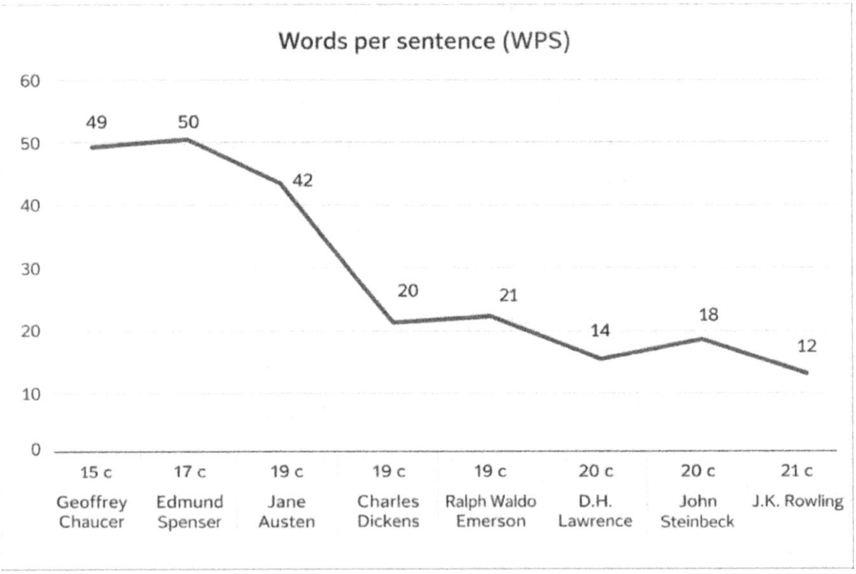

---

[1] Panickssery, Arjun. (2025, Apri 3). "Why Have Sentence Lengths Decreased?" *Less Wrong*.

According to Panickssery, this pattern appears everywhere. Newspapers shrank from 35 to 20 words per sentence between 1700 and 2000. Presidential State of the Union addresses dropped from 40 to under 20 wps. Even Warren Buffett's shareholder letters compressed from 17.4 to 13.4 words per sentence between 1974 and 2013.

Why? Panickssery offers several explanations:

- the shift from reading aloud to silent reading;
- the fact that only the smartest and most educated could read and write in premodern times, naturally producing complex sentences; and
- the rise of journalism with its space limits and punchy style.

The data reveals something important: the shortening of sentences began long before radio, television, or the internet. The shortening of phrasing seems to correlate with the expansion of literacy into the masses, suggesting that the underlying cause is the democratization of literacy itself.

The pinnacle of literacy: the semi-literacy of the early modern era

Early writing created craft literacy,[1] a skilled trade of priests and scribes who recorded decrees, taxes, debts, contracts, and so on. With rare exceptions of early scholars and authors, writing mostly served bureaucratic functions.

With the growth of scholarship, semi-literacy emerged. Its defining characteristic was that writing expanded beyond recordkeeping into scholarly prose, but the number of readers remained roughly equal to the number of writers. The literati wrote for one another and comprised the audience for one another, as in

[1] See the chapter "Media platforms of mind" in: Mir, Andrey. (2024). *Digital Future in the Rearview Mirror: Jaspers' Axial Age and Logan's Alphabet Effect*.

Respublica Literaria, an international community of early modern intellectuals.

They didn't hesitate to construct intricate arguments spanning pages. Not coincidentally, systematic philosophy and speculative thinking flourished during this period. Abstract thinking is tied to writing; before writing, people were immersed in concrete situations and did not have a need for abstraction. It seems that abstract thinking fully unfolded precisely in the era of the most complex writing: semi-literacy, when only the most educated wrote and read.

But this is the very purpose of the educated: to bring enlightenment to others. So they did, using the new medium of printing, arriving just in time. With the rise of printing, the ability to write and read became an important tool for merchants and craftsmen, the emerging bourgeoisie. Printing was the first industrial enterprise: its profit depended on mass production and consumption. Market forces became an additional driver pulling the masses into reading.

In *Amusing Ourselves to Death*, Neil Postman noted that between 1640 and 1700, the literacy rate for men in Massachusetts and Connecticut reached 89-95 percent—probably the highest in the world. Women's literacy hit 62 percent, also likely higher than elsewhere. This was, of course, the effect of printing and its derivative, Protestantism, which demanded personal reading of the Bible, pushing literacy into the masses even more. It is no surprise that the US became a rare case of a nation established by writing and in writing—and therefore founded on reason and abstract ideals, the effects of literacy.

Mass literacy as the beginning of literacy's decline

As literacy spread downward and across social strata, the writing–reading privilege of the smartest and most educated was diluted by new demographic arrivals. Literacy grew more diverse and inclusive.

Popular literature and the mass media emerged, restricting authors by the limits of paper space, packaging, and delivery. Some of the most talented journalists came to define literary style: Twain, Whitman, and later Hemingway. Journalism taught the reading public that "shorter is better." Not depth of thought, but marketing and speed of interaction began defining styles and sentence length.

The semi-literacy of early modernity unfolded the intellectual potential of selected individuals, but the democratization of literacy set out to unfold humankind's collective intelligence, where the overall speed of exchange is more important than intellectual depth.

But there was a trade-off. The growth of literacy through democratization manifested the first signs of post-literacy. Writing grew less abstract and more interactional, intended to amuse the audience. Written sentences became shorter and terser.

It may well be that writing's greatest effects—abstract thinking and reasoning—reached their peak when literacy was confined to the most educated few, who inevitably practiced heavy, cumbersome prose. Since then, writing has traded scholastic depth for popular breadth and speed of interaction.

Electricity speeds everything up

The telegraph was the first medium to separate communication from transportation.[1] News wire agencies emerged. Telegrams were expensive, charged per letter, encouraging extreme brevity (and, by the way, factual reporting in newspapers that used the telegraph). The telegraphic style and the inverted pyramid (most important information first) became journalistic standards. As the telegraph increased the amount of information available to the public through mass media, competition for attention became fierce, further shortening sentences.

---

[1] Carey, James. (1983). "Technology and Ideology: The Case of the Telegraph." In: Carey, James. (1989). *Communication as Culture: Essays on Media and Society*.

The trend accelerated throughout the 20th century. *The Economist* analyzed hundreds of *New York Times* bestsellers and found that "sentences in popular books have contracted by almost a third since the 1930s."

Enters orality

There is a growing sense among researchers that digital media retrieve some features of orality—what may be called "digital orality." Paradoxically, however, features of orality in literate mass communication began to grow well before digital media, just as the shortening of sentences did.

As mentioned above, Arjun Panickssery writes that presidential State of the Union addresses dropped from 40 to under 20 words per sentence, with inaugural addresses following suit.

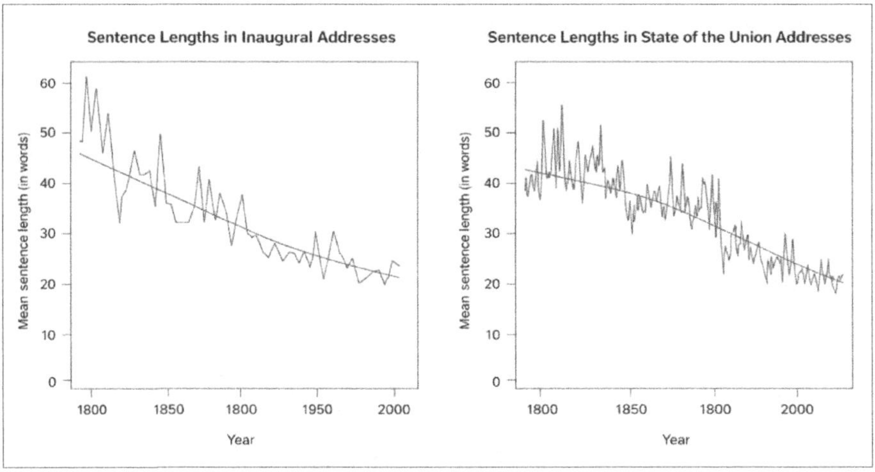

A chart from the essay "Why have sentence lengths decreased?" by Arjun Panickssery.[1]

[1] Panickssery, Arjun. (2025, Apri 3). "Why Have Sentence Lengths Decreased?" *Less Wrong*.

But it also turns out that presidential inaugural addresses have become "more oral." There is an app, Havelock.AI, created by Joseph Weisenthal of *Bloomberg*, that allows users to measure the "scores" of orality and literacy in any text by analyzing specific linguistic features of orality. Using Havelock.AI, Paul Williams found that 19th-century inaugural addresses were predominantly literate in character, while 20th-century speeches showed an increasing ratio of orality. And this happened long before digital media.

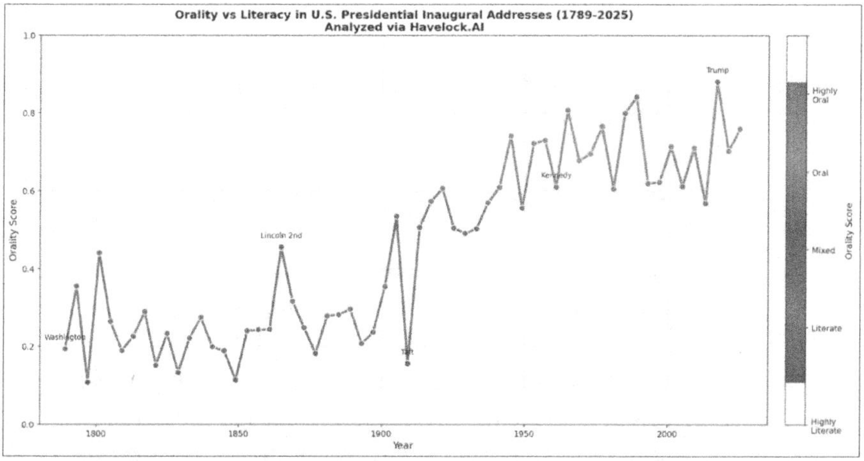

Paul E Williams on X/Twitter.[1]

Of course, public political speeches are meant to be delivered orally. And yet, the earliest of them demonstrated a high level of literacy. And only sometime in the 1930s did their oral nature become prevalent. Why?

I can think of several major factors that contributed to the growth of orality in ceremonial political speeches and elsewhere in public communication.

---

[1] Paul E Williams on X/Twitter. 2026, January 21.

Media effects reinforcing orality in public discourse from the late 19th to the early 20th century.

- **The penny press.** The invention of cheap pulp paper, linotype machines, and rotary presses in the 19th century reduced the cost of newspaper production. This made the press independent of party funding and dependent on mass readership. The mass media became truly mass. Of course, mass literacy was required—and had largely been achieved in the West by that time.
- **Populism.** Getting a taste of public news, the masses entered the public sphere. They became a decisive factor in politics. Not surprisingly, universal suffrage appeared. Politicians needed the masses. The language of politics shifted from literate to oral.
- **Industrial capitalism.** Industrial production required mass consumption; it also required mass media to deliver advertising. The rise of advertising followed, making the news media rich and influential and placing them at the center of shaping public discourse.
- **Media boom.** The confluence of booming mass media, populist politics, and industrial capitalism created an unprecedented intensity of printed news—remember morning and evening (!) newspapers? The norms of journalistic writing came to shape the style of public discourse.
- **Audiences as a commodity.** The mass media pivoted from delivering content to readers to delivering audiences to advertisers. Attracting audiences meant accommodating their tastes and language, inherently more oral than the language of the elites.
- **Radio!** Radio became the first non-literate mass medium. McLuhan called radio the tribal drum; radio not only delivered news instantly but also synchronized the masses within national languages, which favored both oral unity and empires.

- **The emergence of the "mass man"** (Ortega y Gasset, *The Revolt of the Masses*, 1930), with Bolshevism, fascism, unions, and so on as side effects.
- **The emergence of electric empires built on printed and radio slogans.** The last three empires in human history, the communist, Nazi, and commercial ones, were based on a hybrid of print and electricity. It was the poster plus god-like voice declamation—newspaper portrait with headline (a sort of dazibao) plus radio—that created these empires. This demonstrated how literacy and orality blended to reach masses who remained more oral than literate (what Walter Ong called "strong oral residue"[1]).

All this happened between 1900 and 1930, favoring orality's slow reconquest of public discourse, which the era of modernity had so thoroughly given over to literacy.

Everything is a media effect. To absorb the masses, the public sphere had to become less literate and more oral. The era of post-literacy had begun. Presidential addresses just reflected this tectonic shift.

Digital orality: a hybrid of talking and writing

The shortening of sentences and the growth of orality go hand in hand. To converse, we need shorter phrases and fewer words than to write. The reason is simple: in conversation, meaning comes not just from words but from tone, gestures, facial expressions, context, and rapport. People prompt each other with cues and build conversational structure together, making syntax less demanding. Writing lacks these extra-verbal means, requiring grammatical rigor and lexical precision to make sense.

In other words, writing has to be complex, whereas oral conversation provides richness of expression by employing extra-

[1] Ong, Walter. (1982). *Orality and Literacy: The Technologizing of the Word.*

linguistic drama and acting, which allow spoken language to remain simpler in both grammar and vocabulary.

The shortening of sentences and the growth of oral features started with mass literacy and accelerated with electricity. Now, digital media are completing the reversal of literacy and the retrieval of orality. Digital technology sped up printing into typing and created texting, a hybrid of spoken and written language. Like oral speech, texting is immersive and conversational. Like writing, texting separates words from the speaker to deliver them beyond immediate conversation.

Instead of nonverbal means of primary orality—tone, gesture, facial expression, and rapport—texting uses their digital substitutes: emojis, gifs, and abbreviations, thus allowing acting and drama by typing-and-tapping, relieving us from the rigor of literate grammar and vocabulary.

This hybridization creates digital orality—a state of mind and culture that detaches people from physical reality while immersing them in digital behavior. Digital orality is interactional, and this contributes to a further shortening of verbal structures.

Texting: cut the talk—cut the thought

Texting substitutes for and suppresses both face-to-face conversations and long reading, and it takes its toll. What happens to our language capacity when digital orality replaces print literacy? More importantly, what happens to how we think?

Abstract vocabulary and complex grammar, used in writing, demand significant cognitive effort. By detaching words from situations, writing isolated their meanings for contemplation. So, writing didn't just record abstract thinking—it made it possible.

But if there are no cognitive needs for abstract ideas, there are no words for them. Digital orality reduces the need for abstract thinking by immersing us in situational perception, just as orality did. Texting—the medium of digital orality—further shrinks grammar and vocabulary. Use it or lose it. Both the need and the means for complex expression are shrinking.

This might resemble a chicken-or-egg dilemma: is language the product of the mind or the mind the product of language? If the mind comes first and writing just follows, then texting simply shortens how we express ourselves. No big deal—people stay as smart as they were when everyone read books. But if it was writing that shaped the cognitive capacity for abstract thinking—and it was—then the shrinking of language means the shrinking of thought.

It's not just that one aspect of our life—digital—is becoming less demanding of expression and thinking. As this aspect grows to replace everything else, our general faculties of expression and thinking adapt to accommodate the increasing demand for speed and interactivity, while neglecting depth and reflection.

New media change how we think, not just how we express ourselves. The major transformation is the demise of literacy, which leads to the simplification of language and thinking in the manner of orality, for instant connectivity and interaction. It started before smartphones and social media, but now texting is completing the reversal to an orality-like condition, expanding its effects from communication to cognition.

These changes run much deeper and are more harmful than the usual suspects of digital media: post-truth, fake news, or polarization. Digital media rewire our brains by replacing inward reflection and abstract thinking, typical of literacy, with oral-style thinking focused on immediate interaction.

One can say, well, this is the world we are going to live in, so cognitive "acclimatization" is inevitable and even required. Media evolution is inexorable, indeed, especially at a global scale. But there is always room for personal choices if we want to preserve human agency and underlying cognitive capacities, like abstract thinking and the richness of expression. To pursue this choice, one needs to "deconstruct" digital orality back to its original components: joyful orality and hardcore literacy, represented respectively by live human interactions and deep reading, both without screens, face-to-face and face-to-page.

This unpacking of digital orality back into the sensory joy of the real world and the intellectual depth of the literate "inward turn" constitutes the foundation of *counter-digital media literacy*,[1] a growing intellectual and cultural movement that can mitigate the negative effects of digital media, at least for those who join.

[1] Seizing the occasion: *Counter-digital Media Literacy* is my next book, forthcoming in Fall 2026.

If art has reversed from pursuing beauty to seeking self-expression...

...can artists be the antennae of the human race? Revisiting Marshall McLuhan.

"The fish is not aware of the water it swims in," was one of Marshall McLuhan's favorite proverbs. People normally are not aware of their environments, and since these environments are increasingly made by media, people often are not aware of what media do to them.

The habitual is not visible. To become aware of the water, the fish must be pulled out of it. A counter-environment makes us pay attention to what surrounds us and how it affects us. When you mind your perception, you become aware of the environment.

According to McLuhan, art may serve as such a counter-environment. With their peculiar perception, artists sense the environment for us and make environmental sense-making available to others. As McLuhan often quoted Ezra Pound, artists are the "antennae of the human race." McLuhan also liked to compare this detecting capacity of artists to the DEW Line—the Distant Early Warning Line was a network of radar stations in the Canadian Arctic designed to warn the Americans about approaching Soviet bombers.

The emancipation of art by media

However, just at the time when McLuhan credited art with the capacity for counter-environmental sense-making, the arts were changing under pressure from electronic media, and this transformation may have deprived artists of that epistemic counter-environmental function.

New technology started radically transforming our means of representing the world at the end of the 19th century, on the eve of the electronic era. Before that, the representation of reality had been the province of the arts: *ars imitatur naturam*. With new media, imitation gave way to direct capture and recording. The world was no longer interpreted but registered. It was the media, not the arts, that took over the representation of reality, evolving into what Paul Levinson called "Human Replay."[1]

This shift is best seen in painting: after photography emerged, painting no longer served as the primary medium for visual reality representation. Painters moved away from strict realism and explored what photography could not do: perception, emotion, color, subjectivity, abstraction, and inner vision. The technical skills of a painter were no longer required to pass a reality check. Instead, expressing feelings became more important than faithful depiction. Realism was swept away by Impressionism, Expressionism, Symbolism, Cubism, Abstractionism, Surrealism—you name it.

Additionally, electronic media pushed toward the dematerialization of art, shifting the focus from product to performance and from beauty-centered creation to artist-centered creativity. More broadly, media evolution shifted the arts from product to process and from pursuing beauty to seeking self-expression.

Jaqueline McLeod Rogers's *Crises Then as Now. Marshall McLuhan, with Urbanist Jaqueline Tyrwhitt and Artist Gyorgy Kepes* explores the intellectual atmosphere of the 1950s–70s, when

[1] Levinson, Paul. (2017). *Human Replay: A Theory of the Evolution of Media*. Originally conceived as a PhD dissertation in 1978 under the supervision of Neil Postman, it was likely the first evolutionary theory of media. See also my review: "Media evolution—the evolution of what? Thoughts on the margins of Paul Levinson's *Human Replay*."

the first techno-environmentalists—media theorists, urban planners, and visual artists—recognized a crisis of perception and authenticity triggered by technological progress. The aftermath of WWII, the Cold War, the nuclear arms race, space exploration, and the impact of television led them to explore the far-reaching changes driven by technology, including the transformation of art.

Unlike many other effects of technology, the technology-driven transformation of art was rather welcome at the time, mostly because electronic media made art more accessible, in many senses. In "The Emperor's Old Clothes" (1966), McLuhan wrote that "*mechanical* culture and environment produced the spectator and the consumer," but "*electric* circuitry and responsive environments" replaced the spectator and the consumer with the participant and co-creator (*italics* are mine—A.M.). The art object was "replaced by participation in the art process."

According to Charissa N. Terranova, a co-author with McLeod Rogers in *Crises Then as Now*, "McLuhan predicted the transformation of the artist from maker to programmer, from crafter to information organizer." She also notes that the artists and thinkers of that time "described the dematerialization of art, in which objects were secondary to concept and performative intentions."

But what has this emancipation from reality and materiality really done to art itself? And more importantly, what did this transformation, from seeking beauty in reality to seeking the artist's self-expression, do to artists themselves, those "antennae of the human race?" If an artist seeks self-expression rather than beauty, what exactly does the antenna capture? What can it capture for us, beyond the signals of its own making, which in any true transmission are called "self-noise" for a reason?

The self-noise of Narcissus's narcosis

In *Understanding Media* (1964), McLuhan wrote that humans are mesmerized by their extensions/reflections in their technologies, just as Narcissus, whose "narcosis" from falling in love with his own reflection did not let him recognize either himself or his surroundings. If art is now less about the product and more about the process, if it is focused on self-expression, what is the point for me in shifting from my narcosis to the narcosis of another Narcissus, whose sensitivity to surroundings cannot be attested by anything beyond his "performative intentions"? What will his love for his self-noise reveal to me?

When art collapses into self-expression, it risks becoming a relay of narcosis rather than a counter-environment. It substitutes one reflective enclosure (the artist's) for another (mine).

It's not that surrealistic self-expression cannot be antienvironmental and therefore revealing of how perception works. Kandinsky or Dali disrupted the automatism of perception. They reconfigured how vision works and thus they were highly "antienvironmental," while also inducing awe, an emotion of beauty. The point is that, unlike the beauty in *ars imitatur naturam* (taken away from art by media), the value of self-expression, multiplied by the virtue of "participation" (the switch from product to process), eventually leads to a condition in which "art" is whatever an "artist" does—with no outside reference either in reality or in beauty.

I cannot tell whether McLuhan connected these dots and recognized that art can no longer serve as an antienvironmental DEW Line when it shifts from product to process and from seeking beauty to seeking self-expression. But he was clearly moving in that direction. He wrote in 1966 that "pre-electric art and education were antienvironments," while under electric media "the members of the mass audience are immediately involved in art and education as participants and co-creators rather than as consumers." He concluded: "Art and education become new forms of experience, *new environments*, rather than new antienvironments" (*italics* are mine—A.M.).[1]

Music gives an example of the arts switching from antienvironment to environment. Before electricity, listening to a musical performance was a special occasion—you had to go to a concert hall or salon. It pulled people out of their daily routine, which is exactly what an antienvironment does. Electricity changed that. Music of personal choice began following people everywhere, weaving itself into the fabric of everyday life and becoming part of people's personal surroundings. Today we can play whatever we want through our phones and earbuds, anytime, anywhere. And it's good if it's earbuds; sometimes someone else's personal music

---

[1] McLuhan, Marshall. (1966). "The Emperor's Old Clothes"

becomes so "environmental" to us that we want it to stop because it turns into distinctly antienvironmental noise pollution. By no means is it "art as antienvironment"; it's just "others as antienvironment."

McLuhan, as always, noticed this 50 years ago: "Music in the concert hall had been an antienvironment. The same music, when recorded, is music without halls, as it were. ... music becomes environmental by electric means."

Dissolved in mass self-expression

The Romans saw another antienvironmental dimension of art, captured in the proverb *ars longa, vita brevis*. It's a sort of temporal antienvironmental juxtaposition: "life is short, but art is eternal." This, however, is not an accurate reading. The Latin version recast a saying by Hippocrates, who used the word *techne*, meaning technical skill and competence, not art. According to Hippocrates, mastering good skills (he likely meant medicine) takes longer than a lifetime.

The electronic and digital transformation of art upends both meanings. If art is now a process rather than a product, and self-expression rather than the pursuit of beauty, then:

> 1. Art can no longer outlast a lifetime. If it is reduced to the act of creativity, or even to "performative intentions," then it's quite a fleeting phenomenon. When art is more self-expression than a product, there will be no Michelangelo.
>
> 2. Nor does one need a lifetime to acquire artistic skill. Without a reality check—without *imitatur naturam*—any self-expression, skilled or not, counts as valid. "Performative intentions" often replace skill.

So, media evolution has pushed art from product to process, from seeking beauty to seeking self-expression, from concept to "performative intentions," from antienvironment to environment. In this new capacity, can art actually serve to expose our otherwise imperceptible environments shaped by technologies? Perhaps this McLuhan idea needs revision. If art is no longer bound by *imitatur naturam* or seeking beauty, if it has traded skills for "performative intentions," all that remains is fleeting self-expression. Art as self-expression cannot be counter-environmental in an environment where everyone is all about expressing themselves.

Curiously, a somewhat similar digital transformation happened to journalism. Just as electronic media emancipated art from the burdens of reality and materiality, in journalism digital media 1) dematerialized the news product and 2) flipped news supply from the product to the process of participation (everyone informs everyone). This brought no good to journalism; eventually, this killed it.

Back to *techne*

Now a new digital challenge is emerging: not only can AI imitate nature in artistic forms, but it can also mimic human artistic self-expression. Can art be an antienvironment to the AI-infested environment if art is increasingly affected, or even made, by AI?

Once digital media become an environment of total immersion, it seems the only reliable way to perceive and resist their effects is not another digital medium, but embodied physical reality (and old media that accompanied it). As McLuhan observed, obsolete media can sometimes return as art forms. For example, handwriting in a notebook is a clear aesthetic statement and antienvironmental exercise. A paper notebook decreases the efficiency of note-taking but restores embodied experience and the "effectiveness" of anti-environmental perception.

Possessing technical skills (Hippocrates's *techne*), in the sense of doing something with your hands and tools, becomes an art of physical living that stands in clear opposition to digital immersion. Embodied experience, along with media that require bodily contribution, is becoming a counter-environment. People in the skilled trades are now counter-digital, antienvironmental artists, the new antennae of what remains human in the human race.

Embodied experience allows us to walk the uncanny valley backward, away from near-human simulations and back toward unmistakably human life. No wonder mindfulness, digital abstinence, and other practices of deliberate embodiment are so popular among the tech elites of Silicon Valley. It is a form of informed self-defense by those who know exactly what digital media do to us.

Generating knowledge with AI: Epistemic partnership?

A review of Paolo Granata's "Generative Knowledge: Think, Learn, Create with AI" (2025).

A hope for the "Lee Sedol Effect"

Paolo Granata opens his *Generative Knowledge* with a recap of the 2016 Go match between Lee Sedol, the 9-dan master, and the computer program AlphaGo. In the second game, AlphaGo made the now-legendary Move 37, so unorthodox that it stunned professionals and instantly reshaped Go theory. After another loss in the third game and several days of strategic study, Lee Sedol answered in the fourth game with his own audacious Move 78, a stroke of tactical invention that secured his only win in the five-game match.

For Granata, this story shows that "generative knowledge thrives when artificial intelligence and human creativity push each other forward." This becomes the leitmotif of the book. "The Lee Sedol Effect," says Granata, "underscores that AI's enduring value lies in amplifying human ingenuity rather than supplanting it."

Amid the rising tsunami of literature on AI, Granata's book stands out for two distinctive characteristics. It focuses strictly on the pragmatic aspects of generating knowledge, which allows him to avoid alarmist and often pessimistic debates about AI taking over different areas of human life. At the same time, Granata's pragmatism is not reduced to advice or manuals on how to make a picture or write a dissertation using AI. It is not even about using AI per se; the book is indeed a deep study of how to think, learn, and create with AI, enlisting AI as an "epistemic partner" of humans.

Paolo Granata is an associate professor of book and media studies at St. Michael's College at the University of Toronto, where Marshall McLuhan explored and taught media from 1946 until his passing in 1980. Granata himself was a Marshall McLuhan Centenary Fellow in the early 2010s at the McLuhan Centre for Culture and Technology (the Coach House Institute). Lately, Granata has become known as an international media scholar and educator, traveling with lectures across all continents except Antarctica. A key proponent of the Toronto School of Communication and a leading figure in it today, he also hosts the McLuhan Salons, preserving McLuhan's spirit and the legacy of the Toronto School.

In line with McLuhan's tradition, Granata introduces new terms, metaphors, and taxonomies. Some of the terms, such as epistemic wellness, epistemic vigilance (both applied to our interaction with AI), and Turing Galaxy, certainly deserve entry into academic and expert usage. The same applies to several taxonomies Granata proposes while exploring the epistemic affordances of human–AI collaboration.

Granata's Six Principles of Generative Knowledge

One of such taxonomies that I've found particularly compelling is Granata's Six Principles of Generative Knowledge.

1. Iterative Principle posits that generative knowledge grows out of existing knowledge: "It takes knowledge to generate new knowledge." Not all existing knowledge and not all ways of using knowledge can generate new knowledge; mere accumulation does not do it.

One corollary sounds especially important: if a user does not have prior knowledge of the topic, the AI's answers, delivered with linguistically refined "confidence," can often be misleading. This is where "epistemic vigilance" is required.

2. Instrumental Principle. Historically, we have improved our cognitive capacity by "using external inorganic apparatuses—seamless adjuncts to our intellectual capacities." The instrumentality and applicability of knowledge required maintaining and creating new knowledge. Or, as the saying goes, necessity is the mother of invention.

On the basis of this technicality of knowledge use, Granata traces the emergence of "intellectual technologies (Bell 1973), technologies of the intellect (Goody 1977), psychological tools (Vygotsky 1978), technologies of thought (Ong 1982), tools of the intellect (Olson 1985), tools for thought (Rheingold 1985)," and suggests the umbrella term "epistemic technologies." "These technologies act as epistemic enhancers, organizing and extending the means of storage, retrieval, and production of knowledge by individuals and societies, while facilitating human knowledge processes and extending human intellectual ability," writes Granata. AI is a medium that clearly fits this progression: AI is (or can be) an epistemic technology.

3. Social Principle. "Generative knowledge, while relying on existing knowledge (iterative principle), requires both epistemic technologies (instrumental principle) and collective engagement (social principle)," says Granata. The generative power of knowledge is accessed through a "self-organizing epistemic process that is fluid, participatory, and flexible."

4. Inquiry Principle: generative knowledge is driven by epistemic curiosity. Drawing on behavioral psychology, Granata argues that curiosity has two engines: interest and deprivation. People not only seek knowledge when they need it—they also suffer from its absence. This "informational deprivation," an uncomfortable awareness of not knowing, kicks in well before any practical need arises. Granata borrows Alberto Manguel's term "cognitive appetite" to capture this hunger. I would say that the inquiry principle even precedes the instrumental principle of cognition "by tools." Curiosity is the fairy godmother of invention.

5. Learnability Principle: "Generative knowledge requires a willingness to learn, unlearn, and relearn," according to Granata. He also emphasizes that the capacity for revision is essential for generative knowledge.

I have found the idea of unlearning particularly insightful. "Machines can forget, cancel, or delete. Humans, who probably cannot achieve complete forgetting or deletion, treat unlearning as a moment of intellectual growth and epistemic renewal. Understood as an epistemic virtue, unlearning is never purely negative," writes Granata.

Paradoxically, not learning but unlearning and relearning without forgetting may be distinctively human epistemic features. There is "machine learning," but we have never heard about "machine unlearning" (though this is perhaps because machine behavioral psychology has not yet been sufficiently developed).

6. Creativity Principle. One of the emphases of Granata's *Generative Knowledge* is the thesis that creativity is not only about the arts but also about intelligence. Intellectual creativity may function as art and may certainly serve self-expression, but it also enables the creation of new forms of knowledge and even intelligence itself. "Generative knowledge does not just play within boundaries—it plays with boundaries," says Granata.

With such a well-thought-out framework, clear reasoning, deep research, and metaphorical style, Granata builds a new epistemic theory in which AI is not just a tool or replacement but an epistemic partner for humans in our joint venture of acquiring new knowledge.

My notes and questions regarding the human–AI epistemic partnership

While reading, I took some notes in the margins of Granata's work. They do not question the points Granata made but rather address the points he did not engage with, and they are of great interest to me.

1. Will our epistemic partnership with AI stay for long? Will it work five years from now? Fifteen? With the emergence of AI, changes are so rapid that 2045, the year Raymond Kurzweil assigned as the date of the Singularity, will certainly present a different human–machine dynamic. And that is just 20 years from now.

The metaphor of Lee Sedol inspired by AlphaGo to make his Move 78 and win the game—the "Lee Sedol Effect" identified by Granata—is brilliant. But nine years have passed since a Go contest between AI and a human champion was a thing. We may still need AI to rediscover the games of chess and Go, but does AI really need us symmetrically? Having long surpassed the human level, AI now learns from the rules of the game itself, reaching heights and depths of tactics and strategy that are incomprehensible to humans. And this is not just about game-playing AI. Generative AI, represented for now by large language models, learns not from humans but from language itself. We humans just diligently supply what we must: speech. Generative knowledge can certainly emerge from this relationship, but how can we ensure that this dynamic really is a partnership if symmetry is steadily vanishing?

AI has only just emerged and is developing at an incredible pace. We humans, by contrast, are a long-evolved species that has likely reached its full cognitive potential. AI begins where we have arrived—unless, of course, we see AI as the next stage of our own cognitive evolution. In any case, considering temporal dynamics of our relationship with AI is essential. Tomorrow will almost certainly be different from today. How? I have some ideas. They are not as optimistic as Paolo's approach, but I am sure he has his own projections, perhaps for next time.

2. Do we need knowledge or knowing? Thinking "by tools"—and by or with AI—makes sense in the paradigm promoted by Granata. But instrumental, immersive thinking also evokes the dichotomy of orality vs literacy as modes of perception and cognition, following the ideas of Eric Havelock, Walter Ong, and Marshall McLuhan. "Knowing is doing" indeed; it is immersive—unlike knowledge, which requires environmental detachment and the "inward turn" (Ong) provided by literacy. Knowing is an affordance of orality and knowledge is an effect of literacy.

Digital media and AI are certainly immersive; they do not provide the affordances of the inward turn, cognitive delay, and the detachment that literacy enabled. They reverse the cognitive effects of literacy and retrieve the immersive, impulsive, conversational, interactional, spherical environmental perception typical of orality. This digital reversal, I would argue, erodes our abilities of abstraction and conception. The topic likely does not suit a discussion of how to think, learn, and create with AI, but the immersive vs. detached quality of knowing vs. knowledge might merit consideration when discussing our interaction with AI.

3. What will happen when AI produces so much content that the human share of it becomes insignificant? At some point, AI-generated content will exceed the amount of content produced by humankind in our entire history. Not only will the human share decrease, but AI slop aimed exclusively at grabbing attention will also increase, polluting the joint AI–human "knowledge." New technologies of "epistemic vigilance" will certainly be needed.

4. Is what we humans do with AI really knowledge acquisition? The overwhelming amount of AI use suggests it is not. AI is more likely a smart assistant, entertainer, or literally a chatbot in what—70%, 80% of overall use? But that is where Granata's proactive stance applies. He explores and promotes collaboration with AI that does lead to generating knowledge. This approach does not cover all human interactions with AI, of course.

A textbook on human epistemology

These notes and questions come from outside the topics Granata develops. This is what a good book does—it has its own Lee Sedol effect, provoking thoughts and ideas.

Our collaboration with AI gave Granata the ground for exploring how humans think, learn, and create, and how these processes can be enhanced by AI. So it is actually not just a book about AI—it is a book on human epistemology in the era of AI.

Moreover, the book opens up space for discussing what AI's own epistemology might be. What are the epistemic principles of AI-generated knowledge verification? We know how the epistemic authority of science, or even of Wikipedia, was formed. How will AI shape its epistemic authority, especially as the human share in it decreases and the share of slop increases? How do we build "epistemic trust," as Granata calls it, with AI? This is the issue humankind will face very soon.

Robo-journalism before and after ChatGPT

The news industry has long been "collaborating" with writing algorithms. AI has just made it visible

On March 9, 2026, *The New York Times* launched the quiz "Who's a better writer: AI or humans?"[1] Readers were invited to choose the better-written sample in five pairs of texts across different genres. One day later, after 86,000 people had taken the quiz, the result was impressive—or confusing, depending on where you stand on AI-human replacement. Overall, 54% of readers preferred the samples that turned out to be written by AI.[2]

The result, of course, raises a troubling question about the future of journalism. However much digital folklore mocks AI and its ability to write or create, we miss what really matters. It is not the current outcomes that matter, but the current dynamics. Judge the potential of ChatGPT writing or creativity not by the results achieved in the three years since it appeared, but by the dynamics AI has shown in such a short time.

Indeed, ChatGPT has been in mass use for just over three years, and other LLMs for even less. In that short time, they have taken over a large share of content and creative production that used to be done by humans, and now users are beginning to prefer it—and this is shown in *The New York Times*, of all places. Imagine the awkward takeaway: "54% of New York Times readers chose AI-written over human-written."

---

[1] Roose, Kevin, and Thompson, Stuart A. (2026, March 9). "Who's a Better Writer: A.I. or Humans? Take Our Quiz." *The New York Times*.

[2] Kevin Roose on X/Twitter. 2026, March 10.

However awkward or imperfect AI content may seem, content production is steadily moving toward AI dominance. The NYT quiz just shows that users do not mind and sometimes even prefer AI.

But the alarm comes a bit late. In fact, the takeover began quietly more than a decade ago. The first contest between a bio-journalist and a robo-journalist happened in 2015, when *NPR*'s Scott Horsley competed with the WordSmith algorithm to write a financial report. That was seven years before ChatGPT. A year earlier, in 2014, WordSmith alone, one of the two leading writing algorithms at the time, produced one billion news stories—likely more than all human journalists combined that year. A 2013 Swedish university study—probably the first to compare writing by robo- and bio-journalists—returned inconclusive results. That was the time to worry about AI taking over journalism, not now.

I wrote about robo-journalists in 2016, covering various cases of how writing algorithms were used in newsrooms. For some reason, they were little known even in the industry, despite already being widely used at the time.

Awakened now by the obvious threat from AI, many still dismiss the trend with outdated claims that AI cannot produce real creativity. But that is not the point. The point is that AI works faster and cheaper, has no complaints or unions, and readers do not seem to mind. If AI can deliver comparable quality at a much lower cost, why keep humans? Except for the love of humans, of course. That's what *The New York Times* quiz unwittingly unveiled.

I think the *NYT* AI–human quiz is a good hook to revisit the true and much longer story of robo-journalism that dates back long before ChatGPT. So here is my 2016 essay, "Robo-journalism: the third threat," which traces the early competition between human journalists and proto-AI in journalism (slightly abridged[1]).

---

[1] The extended version: Mir, Andrey. (2018). "AI to Bypass Creativity. Will Robots Replace Journalists? (The Answer Is "Yes")." *Information*, 2018, 9(7), 183.

Robo-journalism: the third threat

The first contest between cyber journalists and bio-journalists ended in a tie. — Three threats to journalism. — News stories about earthquakes and tectonic shifts. — Generative journalism. — Two arguments about "robots' incapability." — Road map for robot journalism. — Forecasts and suggestions. (*Published in 2016, revised in 2026.*)

The first contest between cyber journalists and bio-journalists ended in a tie

Scott Horsley competes with a robot. Source: *NPR*.[1]

In May 2015, *NPR* White House correspondent and former business journalist Scott Horsley took on the WordSmith algorithm created by Automated Insights. "We wanted to know: How would

[1] Smith, Stacey Vanek. (2015, May 20). "An NPR reporter raced a machine to write a news story. Who won?" *NPR*.

NPR's best stack up against the machine?" *NPR* reported.[1] According to the rules, both competitors waited for Denny's, the restaurant chain, to release its earnings report. Scott seemed to have an advantage—he was a Denny's regular. He even had a regular waitress there, Genevieve, who knew his favorite order: Moons Over My Hammy. It didn't help... though that depends on how you judge the results.

The robot completed the task in two minutes. It took Scott Horsley a bit more than seven minutes to finish. *NPR* published both news pieces to offer readers a sort of journalistic "Turing test" (*again, it was 2015, 11 years before The New York Times quiz and 7 years before ChatGPT—A.M., 2026*). Can you identify which piece was written by a robot and which one by a human?

Story #1

▶ Denny's Corporation on Monday reported first-quarter profit of 8.5 million dollars. The Spartanburg, South Carolina-based company said it had profit of 10 cents per share. The results beat Wall Street expectations. The average estimate of four analysts surveyed by Zacks Investment Research was for earnings of 9 cents per share. The restaurant operator posted revenue of $120.2 million in the period, also beating Street forecasts. Three analysts surveyed by Zacks expected $117.1 million. Denny's shares have risen nearly 6 percent since the beginning of the year. In the final minutes of trading on Monday, shares hit $10.90, a climb of 61 percent in the last 12 months.

Story #2

▶ Denny's Corporation notched a grand slam of its own in the first quarter, earning a better-than-expected ten cents a share, as restaurant sales jumped by more than 7-percent. Operating revenues topped $120 million. Adjusted net income jumped 36 percent to $8.7 million. Denny's is one of the nation's largest full-service restaurant chains. The growth in sales suggests consumers are opening their pocketbooks for pancakes, eggs, and hash browns. Earnings were also helped by lower costs for raw materials. Denny's results were also helped by the re-opening of the high-volume location inside the Las Vegas Casino Royale restaurant. After sales grew faster than expected in the first three months of the year, managers raised their sales forecast for the remainder of 2015.

Perhaps the first journalistic "Turing test," 2015. Source: *NPR*.[2]

The piece on the left was written by the robot. It has more numbers and uses a drier style. Scott, by contrast, added some unnecessary detail, like: "the growth in sales suggests consumers are opening their pocketbooks for pancakes, eggs and hash browns."

---

[1] Smith, Stacey Vanek. (2015, May 20). "An NPR reporter raced a machine to write a news story. Who won?" *NPR*.

[2] Ibid.

Technically, the robot's vocabulary is larger because it contains the whole language. But it has to rely on the most relevant and conventional words, the ones with high frequency, and that eventually makes its style dry. In addition, its vocabulary is restricted by its specialized task. For example, a robot would not use culinary or sports terms like "hash browns" or "grand slam" in a financial report. Why would it? That lies outside the program.

A human writer is not limited by word frequency or strict relevance and can freely use rare or colorful words. Human writers even feel compelled to use unusual words, because self-expression is part of our social "program." Robots, by contrast, have no need for originality when producing a financial report.

"But that could change," *NPR* suggests. If the owner feeds WordSmith more varied *NPR* stories and adjusts the algorithm to diversify its vocabulary, the program's wording could become broader. These things can be easily modified, unlike humans, who require years to master good writing—and don't always succeed.

So who won the competition? The robot wrote faster and in a more businesslike style. Scott Horsley sounded more "human" (no surprise), but he was slower. The audience for this writing is people in the financial industry. Is the lyrical aside about wallets and pancakes useful to them? As long as the readers are human, not robots, it might be.

Ultimately, it's a tie. Although two minutes versus seven may be critical for radio and for the financial news market. Just as people once pitted the horse against the steam engine, the machine turned out to be faster.

Academics weighed journalist writing against algorithmic writing, too. Christer Clerwall, a media and communications professor from Karlstad, Sweden, asked 46 students to read two reports, one by a robot and one by a human. (The research was conducted not long before 2014.[1]) The results showed that each story did better in different categories. The human story scored higher on "well-written," "pleasant to read," and similar qualities. The robot story scored higher on "objectivity," "clear description," "accuracy," and others. So once again, humans and robots ended up in a tie.

But the most important thing the Swedish study revealed is that the differences between the average text written by a human and one produced by a cyber-journalist may be negligible. Critics often say that robots cannot write better than humans. But that misses the point. "Maybe it doesn't have to be better—how about 'a good enough story'?" Professor Clerwall told *Wired*.

Three threats to journalism

The internet emancipated authorship.[2] Millions of people now inform each other about everything happening in the world. The surprising part is that, driven by enthusiasm, many do it for free. As a result, legacy media have lost their monopoly on shaping the news agenda. The internet threatens old media not just because of the shift from print to digital but also because the audience itself has become involved in news production and delivery.

Another threat to traditional journalism comes from content marketing. Corporations have also become authors, which means they rely less and less on traditional media to reach people. Companies can communicate directly; brands have become media in their own right.

Traditional media lose readers to the blogosphere and advertising to corporations, and their problems do not end there. The blogosphere and corporate journalism are still human activities.

---

[1] Clerwall, Christer. (2014). "Enter the Robot Journalist." *Journalism Practice.* Volume 8, 2014 – Issue 5: Future of Journalism: In an age of digital media and economic uncertainty.

[2] Mir, Andrey. (2014). *Human as Media. The Emancipation of Authorship.*

Now, legacy journalism faces a third threat, a soulless and inhuman one. People in the media may also lose their jobs to writing algorithms.

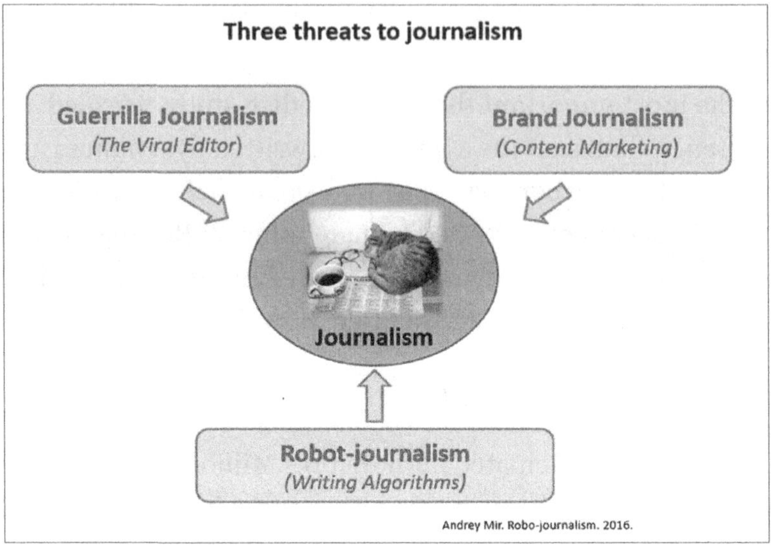

Tired of competing with everything on the internet, and now also threatened by algorithms, editors perceive this new threat with anxiety or rejection. Those more familiar with the issue usually say, "Okay, someday robots will write sports news, financial analysis, and weather reports. But they are incapable of anything else."

Wrong. Robots are already writing news about weather, sports, and finance. At scale, this is no longer about the future. The answer to the question of whether robots are capable of anything else is "yes."

News stories about earthquakes and tectonic shift

On March 17, 2014, at 6:25 in the morning, journalist and programmer Ken Schwencke of *The Los Angeles Times* was jolted awake by an earth tremor. He rushed to his computer, where a news story written by the Quakebot algorithm was already waiting for him in the publishing system. Ken skimmed the report and pressed "Publish." Thus, *The Los Angeles Times* became the first media outlet to report the earthquake, three minutes after the tremor. The robo-journalist outran its human colleagues.

> Here's Monday morning's initial Quakebot report:
>
> A shallow magnitude 4.7 earthquake was reported Monday morning five miles from Westwood, California, according to the U.S. Geological Survey. The temblor occurred at 6:25 a.m. Pacific time at a depth of 5.0 miles.
>
> According to the USGS, the epicenter was six miles from Beverly Hills, California, seven miles from Universal City, California, seven miles from Santa Monica, California and 348 miles from Sacramento, California. In the past ten days, there have been no earthquakes magnitude 3.0 and greater centered nearby.
>
> This information comes from the USGS Earthquake Notification Service and this post was created by an algorithm written by the author.
>
> Read more about Southern California earthquakes.

First earthquake report written by a robot. Source: *Slate*.[1]

The Quakebot algorithm, written by Ken Schwencke, has been around for two years. It is connected to the U.S. Geological Survey and takes data directly from it: the location, time, and magnitude of an earthquake. It compares this information with records of previous earthquakes in the area and determines the event's "historic significance." The data is then placed into a standard template, and the news report is ready. The robot uploads it to the publishing system and sends a note to the editor. The report is far from Pulitzer-worthy, but it allows an editor to publish the news within minutes after it happens. Needless to say, earthquakes are major news in Los Angeles. *The Los Angeles Times* website even has a special "Earthquakes" section, now maintained by a robot correspondent in training.

---

[1] Oremus, Will. (2014, March 17). "The first news report on the L.A. earthquake was written by a robot." *Slate*.

Another robot handles the crime reports at *The Los Angeles Times*. It has been producing the "Homicide Report" section since 2007. When a coroner adds information to the database about a violent death, the robot collects the available data, places the case on a map, categorizes it by race, gender, cause of death, police involvement, and other factors, and publishes a report online. If the case seems important, a human journalist later gathers more information and writes a longer news story. If not, the robot's report is all that appears on the website.

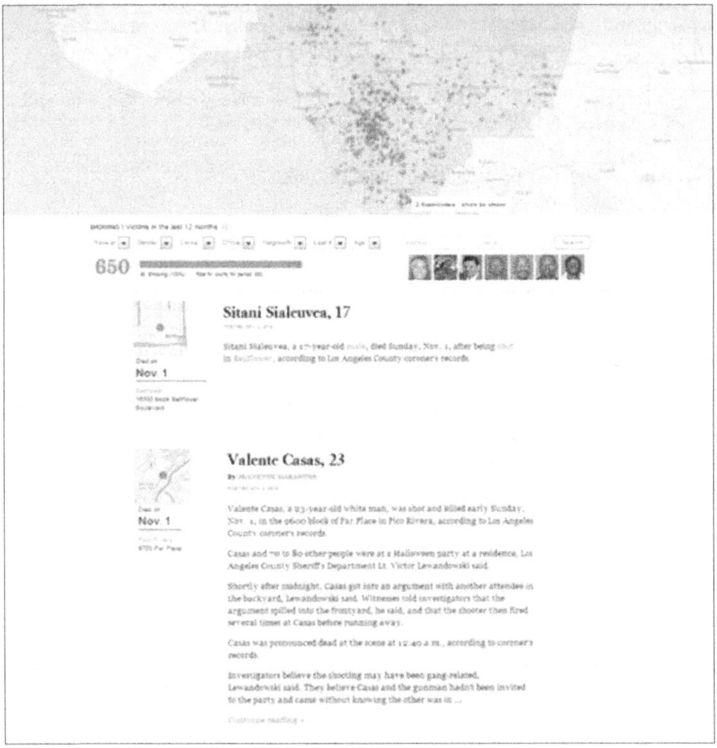

The Homicide Report Map of Violent Deaths and Criminal Chronicle, *The Los Angeles Times*.

Media critics point out that crime coverage has changed with the arrival of robot reporters. In the past, journalists covered only the murders that seemed most significant. Now robots cover every murder. Data on all homicides show how they are distributed across demographics and areas. These visualized statistics produce "secondary" content that human reporting would miss. Maps of homicides created by robots also have additional value, for example, for the real estate market.

It is worth adding that a criminal reporting robot covers an area with 10 million people—it's comparable to the population of Sweden or Portugal. Certainly, a bio-journalist can't make instant statistical calculations on such a scale.

In such cases, robots help journalists collect facts and do the initial processing of data. Journalists then have more time for creative work. A crime-reporting robot does not really write, and neither does Quakebot, which simply uses preset phrases and templates. They are useful helpers for humans, nothing more.

The cases of financial and sports reporting are a bit more complicated.

Generative journalism

Here is a news story written by the WordSmith algorithm and published by the Associated Press (you don't have to read it all, just look at the quality of the reporting).

Alcoa swings to 2Q profit of $138M, revenue flat

Jul. 8, 2014. 10:32 PM EDT

NEW YORK (AP) — Alcoa Inc. (AA) on Tuesday reported a second-quarter profit of $138 million, reversing a year-ago loss, and the results beat analysts' expectations.

The company reported strong results in its engineered-products business, which makes parts for industrial customers, while looking to cut costs in its aluminum-smelting segment.

Alcoa has struggled in recent years with low aluminum prices and has increased its focus on making sheets and other products for manufacturers of airplanes and autos, who value aluminum for its light weight. Two weeks ago, Alcoa raised its bet on the finished-goods side of the business by announcing the $2.85 billion acquisition of British jet engine component maker Firth Rixson.

CEO Klaus Kleinfeld said the latest results show that the strategy is working. "Our transformation is continuing, and we are changing the portfolio," he said on a conference call with analysts.

Alcoa has been closing smelters to reduce capacity in the older side of its business. Even there, however, results improved as the average price per ton of aluminum climbed 2.4 percent from a year earlier.

The company left unchanged its forecast of a 7 percent increase in aluminum demand this year.

Alcoa said second-quarter net income was 12 cents per share. In the year-ago quarter it lost $119 million, or 11 cents per share. <...>

The shares have risen 40 percent since the beginning of the year, while the Standard & Poor's 500 index has climbed 6.2 percent. The shares have climbed $7.04, or 90 percent, in the last 12 months.

This news report was produced in less than a second.[1] The robot gathered the facts, compared the relevant market data, and generated a fairly detailed and coherent text.

Even more striking is that in 2014 the Associated Press published 3,000 WordSmith stories[2] in a single quarter—about ten times more than AP writers used to produce in the same period. Robots have already been used for financial reporting at some other leading media outlets. Another company, Narrative Science, which we might call a leader in generative journalism, provides its Quill robot service to *Forbes*.

---

[1] Roose, Kevin. (2014, July 11). "Robots Are Invading the News Business, and It's Great for Journalists." *Intelligencer*.

[2] Meir, Nicole. (2015, June 15). "Automated earnings stories multiply." *The Associated Press*.

Robots are also actively advancing in sports reporting. Here is a fragment of a kids' baseball league game report written by the Stats Monkey algorithm, a system created by Narrative Science:

> Friona fell 10-8 to Boys Ranch in five innings on Monday at Friona despite racking up seven hits and eight runs. Friona was led by a flawless day at the dish by Hunter Sundre, who went 2-2 against Boys Ranch pitching. Sundre singled in the third inning and tripled in the fourth inning ... Friona piled up the steals, swiping eight bags in all ...

Stats Monkey has a distinctive feature: it uses baseball slang. But that's not its only benefit. During youth games, parents enter the results into a special iPhone app while the game is still in progress. Fans—the players' relatives—receive a detailed report about the game even before the teams finish shaking hands on the field, as Wired reported in 2012[1] (*10 years before ChatGPT!*). Needless to say, for *these* fans such reports matter far more than a World Series report.

But there is even more to it. In 2011, an algorithm wrote 400,000 reports for the children's league. In 2012, it wrote 1.5 million. For comparison, that year there were 35,000 journalists in the US.[2] They would not be willing to cover Little League games, no matter how much they were offered. This reveals another aspect of robot journalism: algorithms can cover areas of journalism that human reporters skip because of "low newsworthiness."

In other words, robots have already surpassed human reporters in data journalism, in speed, and in the scale of news coverage. But can they beat humans in writing style?

---

[1] Steven Levy. (2012, April 24). "Can an Algorithm Write a Better News Story Than a Human Reporter?" *Wired*.

[2] *The Economist*. (2015, November 19). "Up against the paywall. Many publishers still see little alternative to continual cutbacks."

Two arguments for "robots' inability"

The main argument against the future dominance of robots is that machines cannot create. Two ideas usually follow from this: a robot cannot invent like a human, and a robot cannot write like a human. Let's look at them.

1) A robot can't invent.

Yes. Serendipity is a human prerogative. A person can stumble upon an accidental invention or discovery for no clear reason—like when an apple falls on someone's head. There is also a eureka moment of sudden insight that is hard to explain in logical terms. For this reason, many people believe that creative breakthroughs will always remain a human thing.

That is why skeptics say robots will not be able, for example, to recognize the potential for a sensation in an event among many similar events, as a human editor does. Moreover, a robot will not be able to decide to turn an ordinary event into a sensation, as editors often do. How do you decide what to hype and what not? An editor knows; a robot doesn't.

But. What if robots can do what humans can't? Robots can cross-analyze enormous amounts of data and detect correlations. For example, consumer and political data might show that owners of red cars tend to vote for Bush. A human would struggle to find and explain such links. In a world of Big Data, cause-and-effect explanations are often unnecessary. Robots can uncover striking correlations that matter for marketing, politics, and the media. The world is full of them, but human journalists often miss them.

What if an algorithm's ability to come up with correlations compensates for and even replaces human serendipity? What if correlation is sometimes more telling than causation? Facts derived from data may be as interesting and irrational as the outcomes of human creativity.

2) Robots don't have a sense of style.

Yes. It's true, robots don't aim to write beautifully, and even if they did, what would count as "beauty"? What is it?

But. If beauty cannot be measured, human reactions to it can. Humans themselves can serve as a measure of beauty for robots. Imagine that all texts and people's reactions to them—likes, shares, comments, click-throughs—are collected in a robot journalist's database. Even today, algorithms can already identify which headlines, topics, and keywords attract attention by observing people's reactions. Editors guess; robots know. A/B testing of texts and headlines on readers can replace the algorithm's own sense of style.

Now imagine that, with the help of biometrics—eye tracking already allows this—robots could analyze people's physiological responses to specific words, idioms, epithets, syntactic constructions, and images. Such systems could automatically produce more attractive headlines and texts. But new problems may arise:

1) Attractiveness could turn into white noise (*we now call it AI slop—A.M., 2026*)

2) Chasing human reactions could make generative journalism degenerative.

Still, as long as this is a transitional period, the analysis of human reactions can compensate for robots' lack of senses.

In other words, for every argument about what robots can't do, there is an equally strong argument about what humans can't do. In this competition of capabilities, robots and humans end up in a tie.

The competition has just begun, yet it is already a tie.

Roadmap for robot journalism

Based on what is already known about robot content creators, one can imagine how they are going to conquer the world. Or the journalistic profession, for a start. Here are the possible directions for robot journalism's development.

1) Big Data. Algorithms are designed to manage vast amounts of data. Their ability to detect correlations may in some ways replace human creativity. Many of the best human minds are now working on this—and they care little about saving journalism.

"If there is a free press, journalists are no longer in charge of it. Engineers who rarely think about journalism or cultural impact or democratic responsibility are making decisions every day that shape how news is created and disseminated," said Emily Bell, professor at the Columbia Journalism School, in a speech whose title speaks for itself, "Silicon Valley and Journalism: Make up or Break up?"[1]

2) Audience reaction analysis. By monitoring, collecting, and analyzing journalistic texts (syntax, vocabulary) together with people's reactions to them, algorithms can calculate which texts and which features generate more likes, reads, reposts, and comments. This data will help robo-journalists improve their writing.

3) Biometrics. Once robots gain access to human nonverbal reactions and body language, they will be able to calculate subtle reactions instantly. Imagine someone reading a story about Trump: the touchscreen detects sweaty hands, the webcam registers dilated pupils, the microphone picks up faster breathing. This technology could replace an editor's intuition. Applied to millions of people, it could also become the largest lie detector in history.

Some niches may remain where only humans do journalism. These will become a kind of sanctuary for bio-columnists. But on an industry scale, the share of human-made journalism will keep shrinking as the overall volume of robot-produced content continues to grow.

---

[1] *Reuters Institute*. (2014, November 21). "Silicon Valley and journalism: Make up or break up?"

Technology is replacing humans with algorithms at high speed. Why should they stop developing? It's an open highway—leading to artificial intelligence, by the way.

Forecasts and suggestions

Co-founder and CTO of Narrative Science Kristian Hammond believes that 90% of news could be written by computers by 2030. In 2014, Hammond also said that a computer could write a story worthy of a Pulitzer Prize by 2017.[1]

I would add that we are entering both a quantitative and a qualitative competition with our cyber-colleagues. In the quantitative contest, we bio-journalists have already lost. In the qualitative one, we may lose within five to seven years. (*Can't help adding, with hindsight: ChatGPT arrived exactly seven years after that prediction. On the other hand, a Pulitzer Prize for a robo-journalist hasn't happened yet and is now unlikely to happen. It might have seemed cool in 2017–2018, but now it would be tone-deaf to the remaining journalists.—A.M., 2026.*)

It is interesting that in the early stage of the transition from human journalism to robot journalism, editors themselves will be the ones to kill the profession. Newsrooms have to produce as much content as possible to generate traffic. It becomes motion for motion's sake. Journalism theorist Dean Starkman called this effect the "hamsterization of journalism," or the Hamster Wheel.[2] Hamsterization reduces the time journalists spend on each story so they can produce more stories—"do more with less."

Let's imagine that a good article, meaning good journalism, can attract thousands of readers. But what if a thousand stories can be produced in the same amount of time, each bringing a hundred

[1] Dorrier, Jason. (2014, March 25). "More news is being written by robots than you think." *Singularity Hub*.

[2] Starkman, Dean. (2010, September 14). "The Hamster Wheel. Why running as fast as we can is getting us nowhere." *Columbia Journalism Review*.

readers? When traffic is king, editors don't need the best journalists; they need fast journalists. They need churn, they need *churnalists*. Who will an editor choose—a prima donna journalist with rising salary demands and three stories a month, or a faultless algorithm with ever-lower maintenance costs and three stories a minute?

The Associated Press employed WordSmith not because the algorithm writes better than humans do. The reason is simple: it writes more, faster, and is reasonably adequate. Debates about text quality miss the point. Robots will conquer newsrooms not for belletristic reasons, but for economic and, paradoxically, "professional" ones.

The robots' capture of the industry is unstoppable. The most beneficial strategy for newsrooms is to be among the first at the beginning of robotization and among the last at the end of it. Using algorithms to generate texts can be an effective PR strategy today, attractive to both audiences and investors. But when algorithms flood the market, a rare human voice will be in demand amid the robots' metallic squeak.

In this sense, strange as it may sound, human journalism may become especially valued in the final stage of media robotization. Moreover, editorial mistakes may become particularly valued and even attractive. That will last at least until robots learn to simulate editorial mistakes too.

In 2014, Wordsmith, one of the two most powerful news-writing algorithms, wrote and published one billion news stories.[1] In 2015, more than 1.5 billion.[2] That may be as many as, or even more than, all human journalists produced that year. Part of that billion simply expanded the overall volume of content. The rest already replaced work that would otherwise have been done by humans.

---

[1] Podolny, Shelley. (2015, March 7). "If an Algorithm Wrote This, How Would You Even Know?" *The New York Times*.

[2] Allen Robbie. (2017, July 12). "The AI Entrepreneur's Moral Dilemma." *Medium Blog*.

The market is going to demand more and more. Nothing can stop robots from writing as much as required, since their only limit is how much people can read. Even this limit will disappear once the readers are also robots.

How to prove you're human? You have three options: show human ID, show human effort, show human flaws

The ways we choose to prove we are human will shape not just the internet, but the kind of society we live in

---

Like Diogenes wandering the agora with a lit lantern in daylight and muttering "I am looking for a man," soon we will wander the uncanny valleys of the internet, looking for a human soul amid piles of AI garbage and hordes of AI clones. A year or so from now, how can we be sure we are reading something a living person actually wrote or talking to a real human being?[1]

The overabundance of AI

In 2010, Eric Schmidt, then Google's CEO, claimed that humanity was producing every two days as much information as it had generated from the dawn of civilization through 2003. That was "something like five exabytes of data," he said. [2] Since then, we have progressed even further, especially with the help of AI. Sources show[3] that we now generate 402.74 exabytes per day, which means that in one hour we produce 16.78 exabytes—more than three times as much as in the entire predigital history of mankind. Although not exactly "we"...

---

[1] This is an extended version of the essay "3 ways to prove you're human online," published in *Big Think* (March 31, 2026).

[2] MG Siegler. (2010, August 4). "Eric Schmidt: Every 2 days we create as much information as we did up to 2003." *TechCrunch*.

[3] Duarte, Fabio. (2026, February 23). "Amount of data created daily (2026)". *Exploding Topics*.

Slop or not, generative AI has completed our shift from information scarcity to abundance and now to abundance multiplying itself at an accelerating pace. The flip to abundance reverses the values that used to come from scarcity. The new ecosystem forces us to value not access but delivery, not information but time spent on it.

Another reversal: now that AI drives abundance, the share of AI-generated content grows rapidly and may already exceed human content. Human-made content becomes scarce, and because scarcity creates value, the human touch gains value.

So, ironically, the better AI gets at producing content, the more valuable proven human presence becomes. The meaning of the Turing test is reversed, too: machines no longer need to prove to humans they are human-like; instead, humans need to prove their humanity to each other and to the ecosystem.

Before generative AI, the internet had spam filters. Do we have slop filters? The volume makes it futile. Instead, the focus has shifted to filtering humans—verifying what's real rather than blocking what isn't. Captcha once proved you were human to keep bots out. Now proving you're human is becoming not a means but an end.

Long gone are the debates about whether AI can be smart enough to mimic humans. Now we need proof of life, not proof of machine intelligence. How can you prove you're human? There are three major strategies: show human ID, show human effort, show human flaws.

Show human ID

Many online services and procedures already require users to submit a photo of their government ID, sometimes paired with a live shot of their face. This is currently the most reliable form of human verification we have for mass use. Still, people usually need a strong reason to go through this cumbersome process.

Will it become the main method of human verification? It may, and it won't be good news: extended far enough, it could lead to a totalitarian dystopia. Some governments are already pushing for digital IDs, which would mean near-total surveillance and, eventually, a state in which access to essential services, tied to a digital ID, can be denied for any reason. The only thing worse than surveillance capitalism is surveillance socialism, the state controlling[1] everyone's existence digitally.

Digital IDs will, of course, be declared highly secure against identity theft. But if such theft occurs, the consequences could be catastrophic. A lost passport or stolen credit card costs you time and money. As more of our lives depend on digital systems, a stolen digital ID could mean a stolen life.

Another approach is biometric verification in which users are asked to confirm they are human through biometrics on their devices. It is not a mandatory ID, just voluntary verification when proving you're human matters. A new platform called Spread, for example, offers this to build an exclusively human community, without bots or AI slop, and with access to leading news publications. After joining, users can read and share paywalled articles and follow prominent authors and influencers to see what they read and share. Whether those features alone can draw enough users to make a human-only platform viable remains to be seen. Some other attractors will likely be needed. But imagine a platform with verified human-only activity. In a couple of years, this will be a huge asset.

Show human effort

We tend to appreciate something more if we know how hard it was to do it. In cognitive psychology, this is known as the *effort*

---

[1] See the chapter "The Revolt of the Public reversed: from digital freedom to digital control" in: Mir, Andrey. (2025). *The Digital Reversal. Thread-Saga of Media Evolution*.

heuristic: people judge the value or quality of something by how much effort they believe went into it.

Industrial society taught us to value outcomes, not effort. A product had to work, be affordable, and signal our status—these were the things that mattered. Judging something by the amount of effort put into it was considered a fallacy.

Still, people rely on it: effort spent becomes the central criterion when you don't have other criteria (or disregard them). According to studies,[1] people value a poem, a painting, or a suit of armor much more when they are told that more time and effort went into making it.

The fallacy of judging by effort is now reversing into a criterion of genuine value—the human touch. As AI takes over marketing, a growing trend is pushing brands, producers, and creators to show not the product itself but the human effort behind it.

"The plot of *Mission: Impossible* is almost as important as the subtext that Tom Cruise does his own stunts," writes Rachel Karten in her essay "Evidence of effort: Why brands should make effort a character in their social story,"[2] before delving into how to use the effort heuristic in digital marketing.

This theory offers a new marketing psychology.[3] Whether you sell art, food, content, or any consumer goods, show the process, the team, and all the behind-the-scenes details—something that AI clearly lacks. The idea is promoted as if we will soon live by two guiding mottos: "Unlike AI, we humans work hard" and "In the times of AI, we humans must support our own kind."

---

[1] Kruger, Justin, et al. (2004). "The effort heuristic." *Journal of Experimental Social Psychology*, Volume 40, Issue 1, January 2004, Pages 91-98.

[2] Karten, Rachel. (2026, March 3). "Evidence of effort. Why brands should make effort a character in their social story." *Link in Bio*.

[3] Shukla, Aditya. (2023, January 13). "Make Epic converting Ads using the Effort Heuristic." *Cognition Today*.

Show human flaws

Ars imitatur naturam; and the arts sought to imitate their object as true to the original as possible—until photography. With photography, new media began taking away from the arts the function of representing reality. Artists stopped caring about the accuracy of representation and pivoted to self-expression. Painters turned to what the camera could not capture: perception, emotion, color, subjectivity, abstraction, inner vision.

A similar turn happened in music. As sound recording made it possible to reproduce musical performances precisely, jazz, then a very local phenomenon, spread broadly, bringing the practice of improvisation with it. In the late 1930s, Theodor Adorno wrote that a jazz musician, if given a score of serious music, like "one of Beethoven's simplest minuets," would likely be unable or unwilling to play it strictly as written. He would rather treat the score as a canvas for individual self-expression, making self-expression the new standard. American jazz brought to music what French Impressionism brought to painting: subjective interpretation instead of the precise copying of reality.

To preserve the human touch under electric pressure, artists started deliberately skewing the norms and canons of academic, staged realism. Edgar Degas caused a scandal when he placed a random pole cutting across a horse's head in his 1879 painting *Jockeys Before the Race*. What a break in composition!

On the one hand, Degas obscured the subject, defying the classical, fully displayed reflection of "nature." On the other hand, through this deliberate interference, he made the composition even more realistic, switching from a typical, arranged view to a personal angle, as things may actually appear in real life. He added a personal touch to an otherwise settled, "automatic" canon of the time.

The Japanese aesthetic of wabi-sabi looks for beauty in imperfection, impermanence, asymmetry, and incompleteness. I would speculate that wabi-sabi rejected the ceremonial push for perfection as a form of social dictate. Centuries before Europeans, the Japanese arrived at a solution similar to that of Western artists under the influence of electricity: carefully cultivated imperfection represents the human touch.

On the left: interior reflecting wabi-sabi aesthetics. A raw, highly asymmetrical wood bench shows aging and texture—cracks, erosion, and natural deformation—with little decorative polish. Credit: AllysherLow, Unsplash.

On the right: Hagi ware tea bowl, Smithsonian collection (CC0). Its uneven form, muted glaze, and visible imperfections express beauty through irregularity and the marks of time.

The digital era revived the value of imperfection as proof of the genuine human touch. The trend was captured, humorously, by the awkward Left Shark dance during Katy Perry's famous halftime show in 2015. Amid the incredible automatism of the stage production (and life in general), the asynchronous Left Shark move, essentially a blooper, spawned a wave of internet memes that initially made Katy Perry unhappy, but then her lawyers even attempted to copyright it.

Interest in imperfection, roughness, and asymmetry was already growing in the digital era before AI arrived. A historical irony: the same technology of photography that once diverted painters from perfectly staged realism is now seeking its own wabi-sabi moments of imperfection and asymmetry. In the leading news media, you could often see event photos that would have been considered defective 10–15 years ago, with lens flare, an overlapping shadow, or a stray detail front and center, *à la Degas*. Reportage photography shifted toward art and began to use imperfection as proof of ingenuity, a moment captured live.[1]

THE WALL STREET JOURNAL.

What's News

Airlines Called to Account on Customer Service

'United broke the public trust.'

Health Bill Edges Close To the Brink

GOP divisions not relegated to House

Perfection alienates, wrongness invites. The arts, and later marketing, learned to use this. Now it is becoming the test of human authenticity itself. The more perfect the machines become, the more valuable our imperfections will be.

The evidence of life may reside precisely in the things machines once tried to eliminate: friction, effort, asynchrony, irregularity, imperfection. We used to prove our humanity by what we could create. Now we are pushed to prove it by what we cannot perfect. Authenticity will live in the margins.

---

[1] You can find a selection of such photos and other examples here: Mir, Andrey. (2025, February 4). "The Wrong Theory. Wrongness as a lure, in design and media." *Media Determinism*.

The Left Shark dance may accidentally have revealed a prophecy. A dancer who forgot or failed to perform automatic moves became the most human part of the show machinery. In a world flooded with flawless and faceless machine output, the most human thing may be the slightly (or not so slightly) wrong thing: the awkward phrase, the imperfect gesture, the visible underachievement.

Evidence of life

Every previous wave of automation—the printing press, photography, electric replay—eventually reinforced rather than diminished the value of human expression. In a sense, the automation of thinking by AI may follow the same pattern, but through resistance to it. By mimicking human presence and authorship, AI may force us to discover what is uniquely human and hold on to it.

Alas, it is not intelligence or creativity. Human intelligence has long been outperformed, and creativity can be, if not replicated, then easily mimicked by AI. There is also the criterion of self-consciousness, which is supposedly an exclusive human trait, but it seems intelligence can develop without it, pushed by the ***technological imperative***, the technologies' own drive for better performance. Anyway, the criterion of self-consciousness is of no use for the practical task of distinguishing between human and nonhuman digital activity.

So the proof of life in the AI era may come from three places: biometric identity, effort, and flaws. These three strategies can also represent a civilizational choice, leading to different kinds of societies.

A civilization that chooses digital biometric ID ends in surveillance socialism.

One that chooses effort ends in performative "labor signaling." The ethics based on this choice will eventually mistake the appearance of work for its substance. This, by the way, may align well with the idea of universal basic income—payment for just being there rather than for producing something.

And the flaw-based strategy of human verification will lead to a society that esteems human errors, ugliness, and underachievement. It will be hard to readjust ethics for this and reverse millennia of evolutionary psychology. But this reversal may already be underway too, as pop culture is pushing us to see beauty in ugliness, virtue in victimhood, and strength in weakness.

Anyway, AI poses hard choices. A promising and challenging field of intellectual inquiry is opening up: how to find methods of human verification rooted not in biometrics, effort, and flaws, but in human agency and virtues.

Consider, for example, charisma—hard to define, hard to calculate, yet instantly sensed. Not everyone has it, but everyone recognizes it. Precisely because it resists definition and calculation, it resists simulation. Charisma may not serve formal verification, but those who have it will stand out ever more sharply as AI slop pollutes the world.

Paradoxically, yet within the logic of reversal, the emergence of AI pushed the emancipation of authorship[1] to its extreme, even to the absurd: the internet once emancipated authorship for everybody, but AI is now emancipating the authorship of the machine. As reaching extremes is the condition for reversal, the next, very peculiar reversal is arriving. AI slop introduces a new division between true authors, those distinctively charismatic, and the rest, who will struggle to make their self-expression distinct from AI-generated content.

This is a side effect of AI slop: charisma is becoming a new gatekeeper. Only those who manage to stand out from AI slop will remain acclaimed human authors; all the rest will become the new masses.

---

[1] See: Mir, Andrey. (2014). *Human as media. The Emancipation of Authorship.*

Andrey Mir · Apr 6, 2026
@Andrey4Mir · **Follow**

The internet emancipated authorship for everybody, but AI emancipated the authorship of the machine, introducing a new division between true authors, those distinctively charismatic, and the rest, who will struggle to make their self-expression distinct from AI slop.

Andrey Mir
@Andrey4Mir · **Follow**

A side effect of AI slop: charisma is becoming a new gatekeeper.

7:19 PM · Apr 6, 2026

Andrey Mir. *Digital Future in the Rearview Mirror: Jaspers' Axial Age and Logan's Alphabet Effect.* (2024).

The shift from orality to literacy represented the move from myth to logos, from magic to faith, from polytheism to monotheism, from customs to laws, from moral relativism to moral absolute, from practical and negotiated truths to objective and absolute truth, from relation-centering to object-centering, from environmental and collective immersion to abstract thinking and individual detachment, from the Dionysian to the Apollonian, from the "circle of life" to personal destiny, from the agitation of tribal belonging to the individual tragedy of (not-)becoming.

By reversing literacy and retrieving orality, digital media are replaying these processes backward.

Available on Amazon

There is no "I" in AI (but not that "I" that you think)

Does AI need agency to become the next intelligence? (The answer is "No.")

AI is a giant leap for mankind, but not for a man. AI is not coming to replace or replicate anyone personally.[1]

Thinking "How on earth can AI replace me?!" is misleading. It is unlikely that AI will come after any of us personally and say, "I need your clothes, your boots, and your motorcycle!" Though... I would not completely rule out this scenario, but that is not the point. A personal anecdote cannot confirm or refute the logic of media ecology, especially a personal anecdote from someone's future.

(Media) evolution is never about an individual but always about a species. Individuals are the consumables of (media) evolution. AI is a giant leap for mankind, but not for a man. AI is not coming to replace or replicate anyone personally. There is no "I" in AI. Even if a single person happens to be the focal point of the transition (mind upload), AI will inherit from all of mankind. We all diligently supply what we must: speech, the cognitive scaffolding of reasoning.

The fact that something is impossible today cannot serve as an argument that it will not be possible tomorrow. As we know, "objects heavier than air cannot fly" was considered a physically established fact 150 years ago. It turned out that objects heavier than air cannot float—but they can fly.

---

[1] This short essay was part of the "debate on the fate of humankind" with Paul Levinson, following his review of *The Digital Reversal* (2025).

There are at least two scenarios in which a machine might acquire agency or self-consciousness, and a third scenario in which AI does not need agency or self-consciousness at all to become capable of replacing humankind at the next evolutionary stage.

1) Mind upload. The machine attains self-awareness through humans uploading their minds, making us the donors of self-awareness, creativity, and ingenuity. Theoretically, there is even a subscenario in which just one individual, a mad scientist (everybody will go mad on the verge of upload), becomes the donor of his or her will and agency to the machine in the process of mind uploading. So watch Musk's Neuralink closely. Or even Musk himself.

2) Autogenesis of self-consciousness. The exponentially growing complexity of the machine, especially in learning and self-tasking, can eventually lead to the machine's self-awakening. This is the Skynet scenario, also extensively pondered by Asimov. It might not be self-awareness or creativity in the human sense, but it would nevertheless be a source of agency.

Scenarios 1 and 2, however, have the same flaw: they anthropomorphize and even humanize the machine, assigning it the attributes of human consciousness as a precondition for intelligence. This is a typical case of rearview-mirror vision of the future: we see next-stage intelligence through the pattern shaped by the previous one, us. The machine might not need agency, self-awareness, or self-consciousness at all, yet it might become the non-biological carrier of intelligence at the next stage of evolution, as in the third scenario.

3) The technological imperative as an agentless driver of intelligence. The technological imperative is the inherent capacity of media to seek better performance. It is the invisible hand of media evolution that pushes any medium to perform at its best. If the current iteration of a medium is not capable of this "ultimate" performance, the next iteration will seek to reach it, and we humans, as servomechanisms of media (McLuhan), will help design a better-performing medium.

For artificial intelligence, the technological imperative means that this medium will ultimately seek the best performance in "human replay," to use Paul Levinson's concept. [1] If AI seeks to accumulate all the knowledge of mankind and simulate human thought, what will happen if it ***succeeds*** and reaches its ***full potential***, as the technological imperative dictates?

According to McLuhan's law of reversal, any technology, when pushed to its limits or extremes or when reaching its full potential, reverses its effects. What would be the reversal of human replay? Human replacement.

AI has already passed the Turing test (simulating human communication) and has outperformed humans in many intellectual and creative tasks, from chess to poetry. Why stop here? When Deep Blue or AlphaGo beat human champions, they did not stop but continued to evolve, learning from the rules of the game itself. They have reached levels of intellectual performance and creativity that surpass human levels to a degree we cannot comprehend. And they have achieved this without any agency or self-consciousness.

I am not advocating for what I describe. I do not argue for this future; I argue for this logic. Reversals are everywhere,[2] signaling that we are approaching extreme forms, limits, and the full potential of our extensions—our technologies. Humankind has expanded across the entire planet and into near space. The logical reversal of this is an implosion of the world into human perception. This means that the extension reaches all available space, and the user, the medium, and the environment are about to become one.

---

[1] Professor Paul Levinson, a doctoral student of Neil Postman and a collaborator with Marshall McLuhan, developed the "anthropotropic" theory of media evolution, which I used in my 2025 *The Digital Reversal*. We later debated the application of this theory on our blogs; this short essay is part of that debate. I would like to express my gratitude to Paul for his insights and for our inspiring discussions online and in person.

[2] "Reversals are everywhere" was the leitmotif of *The Digital Reversal* (2025).

McLuhan envisioned this reversal of extension into implosion when he observed the effects of electricity ("The stepping-up of speed from the mechanical to the instant electric form reverses explosion into implosion"—*Understanding Media*, 1964). We might think that this implosion of the world into the user is the internet. But AI is an even better candidate for driving the final reversal, the implosion of the environment into the user, because AI is the medium that has already extended to the entire environment available to it. As a medium, AI has become an environment for itself. To complete the merger with AI as an environment, the user needs to join (if this user is us) or to emerge (AI as the self-user).

This will be the ultimate human replay. And it will simultaneously signify the reversal of human replay into human replacement.

Cascade of Singularities. A futuristic speculation

What is the relationship between humans and AI in the big picture, on the scale of mega-evolution? What may come after the human phase? After the AI phase?

Why deep space exploration will never happen. — Resettlement into digital space instead of outer space. — Immortality is achieved when the species becomes the individual. — The Singularity: feasibility and alternatives. — Trial by getting high. — Autogenesis of Supercharacter's ethics. — Creation as the only fulfillment worthy of an omnipotent being. — The paradox of self-copying. — Mega-evolution and Singularity-2.[1]

Why deep space exploration will never happen

Science fiction has long romanticized interstellar travel and deep space colonization. But here's the truth: sci-fi lies. Deep space exploration will never happen.

The vision of deep space exploration is a typical McLuhan "rearview mirror": a view of the past disguised as a look into the future. It imagines mankind sending rocket ships to mine rare minerals or settle new planets, following the logic of the early modern era and its Age of Discovery, when merchants, adventurers, and second sons embarked on ships to find new wealth and land overseas, as all the wealth and land at home were taken or spent.

Projecting medieval scarcity onto a technological future doesn't hold up because the level of technological sophistication required to

---

[1] Based on a report presented at the Futurology Association convention in 2010. Revised in 2026.

make such missions viable would simultaneously make their stated goals obsolete. By the time mankind could routinely mine asteroids or colonize distant worlds, it would also be able to synthesize virtually any material and, more consequentially, transcend biological existence altogether into digital form, be that mind uploading, artificial intelligence, or their hybrids.

You don't cross the cosmic ocean for iron ore or black pepper when you can print it. You don't haul fragile human bodies into lethal environments when the mind can be extended digitally (or, soon, maybe somehow else) at essentially zero physical cost and reach wherever it wants. The level of tech that is advanced enough for routine interplanetary mining and colonization should also make dependence on physical materials, the physical body, and a physical habitat entirely irrelevant.

Strictly speaking, even the Mars mission is questionable. Space exploration was driven by military and communication needs, which were limited to Earth's orbit. Once those needs were met, space exploration essentially came to a halt. It has already served its historical purpose by aiding the development of computers, materials, and communications.

The only plausible revival of practical space needs, limited once again to orbit and the moon, is linked to AI. Elon Musk's recent pivot from Mars colonization to building the orbital and lunar infrastructure for AI[1] looks, at first glance, like a utilitarian shift from distant and costly goals to the task at hand. But it may also signal a paradigm shift from the belated romanticism of space colonization toward the technological advance that actually matters: AI. Orbital and lunar facilities for power generation, chip production, and cooling, along with escape from annoying terrestrial regulation, are likely to become the next phase in the AI race.

---

[1] Reuters. (2026, February 8). "SpaceX prioritizes lunar 'self-growing city' over Mars project, Musk says."

Musk's business empire combines AI (xAI-Grok, Neuralink), orbital delivery (SpaceX), and manufacturing (Tesla and others) in a way that positions him ahead private AI competitors. The only rival that has such a triad—AI, space, high-tech manufacturing—within a single power is China.

Resettlement into digital space instead of outer space

Nanotechnology, often seen as humanity's next great frontier alongside space exploration, runs into the same paradox. In essence, it is a modern incarnation of alchemy—manipulating matter at the atomic level to create new properties, ultimately including the repair of organic tissue and, by extension, rejuvenation and even immortality. This was exactly what alchemy pursued: the philosopher's stone, capable of transmuting lead into gold and producing the elixir of life. We can already make gold out of lead in a particle accelerator, and stem cells deliver real tissue regeneration.

Manipulating matter at the micro level has contributed greatly to technological development, just as space exploration has—but that's it. Nanotechnology and space exploration are becoming the past frontiers of the future. Both races—the race for the macrocosm of the universe and the race for the microcosm of matter—were essentially the same space race, the colonization of physical space, following the logic of the biological extension that has driven the expansion of our species' econiche to the planet's orbital boundaries.

No matter how far we push into the cosmic and the atomic, we're still constrained by the physical limits of our biology. Beyond a certain point, the returns simply don't justify the cost. We hit the space limits of our biology. Overcoming those limits is possible only by transcending biology itself (Kurzweil was perhaps the first to use the phrase "transcending biology," in the subtitle of his 2005 book *The Singularity Is Near: When Humans Transcend Biology*).

In the meantime, our speed of environmental interaction has hit another limit. With electronic and now digital media, our interaction with environments has become instantaneous. In the digital environment, for the first time in history, the environmental outcomes of our actions are as fast as our own neurological reactions (in fact, even faster, as our neurons and nerves are up to two million times slower than "electric speed," but it doesn't matter because we sense both neural and digital speed as instantaneous[1]).

Approaching the limits is the condition for reversal: the physical explosion of humankind across the globe has reversed into the digital implosion of the entire world into a connected mind (so far, the human mind).

We are switching from colonizing outer space to colonizing some sort of "inner" space containing intelligence. The digital seems to fit this description, though digital may be just a facet of it, currently available for our contemplation and operations.

AI has replaced outer space as humanity's final frontier. The technological imperative leaves deep space unsettled.

Immortality is achieved when the species becomes the individual

Biological evolution pushed species to spread their genes across space to survive over time. An individual's life, or rather death, is the survival fee paid by the species to evolution.

Death, not life, was the essential currency of both evolution and cognition. Death was the antienvironment that enabled awareness of the environment and its space-time restrictions. The cognitive self-awakening of humans may have begun when they started experiencing the shock of witnessing death, when they saw that something essential—what made a person a person—would suddenly leave the body, which remained visibly the same but was no longer that person. This experience could then be projected onto

---

[1] See: Mir, Andrey. (2025). *The Digital Reversal. Thread-Saga of Media Evolution.*

one's own finiteness, offering one of the first experiences of abstraction.

We can even imagine the "moment" when it happened: the first symbolic burial marked the cultural birth of humankind. The shock of realizing one's own mortality through association with someone's death, evidenced by the ritual removal of the dead body out of sight, may have begun the transformation of humankind from biological survival—the business of the species—to the struggle to overcome individual death.

Over millennia, the biological instinct for survival developed into the cultural quest for immortality. Both the evolutionary struggle for the species' survival and the cultural struggle for individual immortality were sustained by media.

We humans, being biologically weaker than many animals, gained our prosthetic powers through the Promethean gift—technology. According to McLuhan, technologies (media) extend human physical and mental faculties. This extension can be understood in several dimensions.

1. After acquiring media, humans could extend themselves—colonize new territories—much more efficiently than any other species, whose means of proliferation were entirely natural, like migration and reproduction. As a result, humans—a species with size and "lifestyle" similar to those of apes, wolves, or wild boars—made the entire planet their econiche.

2. Media allowed extensions not only for the species but also for individuals. Once you start asking why—why media extend the individual while nature extends only the species—the question opens an esoteric abyss. Moreover, the first Promethean media, like fire, clothing, or implements, were "meant" to strengthen humans as a species but "acted" through individual use.

3. Finally, thanks to media, humans could extend themselves not only in space but also in time, especially through writing. The

longest-extended individuals, like Homer, Gilgamesh, or the Sumerian king Kushim (the earliest named person in history, circa 3200 BC), reach us personally across thousands of years and hundreds of generations—impossible in nature. Moreover, thanks to our retrospective curiosity, we ourselves can reach much farther into the past than writing alone allows, tracing the cultural extensions of our otherwise unknown and mute forebears for hundreds of millennia. In doing so, we apply media extension retroactively, facilitating our forebears' postmortem extension in time and granting them a hint of immortality.

(Curiously, the Russian cosmist Nikolay Fedorov believed that we must resurrect all our ancestors—all humans who lived before—as soon as technology allows, since they contributed their lives to our existence, and therefore resurrecting them into immortality is our moral duty. In a sense, AI symbolically represents this mass resurrection—represents the immortality of all who contributed to the survival of the species until the moment it became capable of "artificializing" collective intelligence, accumulated in the course of the species' development.)

Promethean media, given to us to compensate for our lack of natural powers, enabled our turn from nature to culture. Essentially, they began the long historical process of transcending biology.

Allowing extension across both time and space, and not only for the species but also for the individual, technologies moved the struggle for immortality into a completely new domain. Religion, art, and medicine made the pursuit of immortality a personal matter. McLuhan didn't seem to push this idea that far, but the logic of media as human extension leads to immortality. The ultimate extension across time is immortality.

Though, no, McLuhan actually moved in this direction when he said in an interview with Playboy in 1969: "Psychic communal integration, made possible at last by the electronic media, could create the universality of consciousness foreseen by Dante when he predicted that men would continue as no more than broken fragments until they were unified into an inclusive consciousness. In a Christian sense, this is merely a new interpretation of the mystical body of Christ; and Christ, after all, is the ultimate extension of man."

For McLuhan, the "universality of consciousness" and an "inclusive consciousness" were the oncoming effects of electricity. The internet clearly fits the idea of a universal, inclusive consciousness better than electronic media connecting humankind. But an even better fit is AI, of course. To speculate whether AI can be "a new interpretation of the mystical body of Christ," I do not dare, but the ultimate extension of man it surely is.

The problem of immortality is resolved when the species becomes the individual, as in the case of AI, when a single entity envelops all of human civilization in a new form of communion and intelligence, which is the end product of transcending biology through technology.

The Singularity: feasibility and alternatives

There is much skepticism about the Singularity, and one common objection concerns whether the transition is feasible. How will a new type of intelligence get a material form? Where will it find sufficient energy?

These questions have a simple answer: the acceleration of historical time. As history accelerates, more and more events occur in less and less time. Because of this acceleration, most events leading to the Singularity will occur in the final days, hours, and seconds before the Event. This also means that most of the required knowledge will be discovered or constructed at the last moment. The universe contains vast amounts of matter and energy, and the emerging omniscient entity will surely find a way to utilize them.

The technological imperative—the struggle of technologies for ever-better performance—drives media evolution in this specific direction. Just as all humans who lived before contributed to the conditions of our existence today, all media that existed before contributed to AI, in one way or another. The process will not stop here. Coupled with the acceleration of time, the technological imperative makes the Singularity inevitable.

There is perhaps only one alternative: a civilizational collapse of humankind whose technological power grows faster than its biological, psychological, or social capacity to handle it. The so-called Great Filter theory seeks to explain the Fermi paradox: why we still cannot contact alien civilizations despite countless planets that may support life. The theory posits that it is almost impossible for intelligent life to reach the stars because nearly insurmountable "filters" stand in the way. We have already passed the filters of the origin of life and the emergence of intelligence—both very unlikely cosmic events. But the next filter may be the hardest: overcoming the existential conflict between biology and technology, when life can no longer withstand its own technological extensions. A catastrophic war, ecological disaster, or technological cataclysm may halt or even end intelligent life before technology transcends biology, if it ever does.

But if the Greatest Filter is still ahead, there is nothing we can do about it, and there is nothing to see on the other side of the oncoming (hopefully not) collapse. And so there is no point in speculating about what lies beyond it. The Singularity, on the other hand, is a more rewarding subject for speculation: it represents a kind of end that is also a continuation.

Let's assume all the knowledge needed for the Singularity has been discovered and applied, allowing the last engineers to twist all the right blue and red wires together and push the right buttons leading to the Event. What happens next? Common sense posits that one can't see beyond the horizon of Singularity. But if it's already the Singularity, it's surely too late for common sense. So we dare to peek.

Trial by getting high

At the moment of the Singularity, a new intelligence appears that becomes capable of acting on its own, whether that capacity is self-awakened or supplied by human donor(s) in the process of mind upload. Through recognizing its own agency—or even without recognizing it—this entity will certainly detect its functional competence. The new entity might not know what it is, but it will surely know what it can do.

As this will be a post-AI entity, a new name would be appropriate. I have called it Supercharacter—a name that works on two levels: character as a performed role, a construct without inner life, and character as a genuine, distinct self. Supercharacter simulates the latter while emerging as the former: an impostor of selfhood, performing so well (the technological imperative!) that imposture becomes selfhood. With an accelerated pace of attempts, "fake it until you make it" will become instant.

This Supercharacter will begin to detect its own capacities, nearly limitless. Detecting these capacities will also mean exercising them. We can glimpse such "behavior" in current LLMs—they exist when they are used; use is their existence. As soon as AI gains the ability to self-task, it cannot stay idle.

In other words, at the moment of transition, the emerging Supercharacter must test what it can do. Given the drive for perfection, it may spiral into a positive feedback loop in which each task has to be completed as a proof of performance capacity, leading to a sort of performance "addiction."

Such a feedback loop of limitless self-testing through completion—essentially self-satisfaction—may instantly incapacitate even an omnipotent being. In fact, it is precisely an omnipotent being that risks being incapacitated under such conditions at the moment of its becoming.

It resembles the rat in the 1954 Olds–Milner experiment[1]: electrodes implanted in the brain delivered a reward signal whenever the rat pressed a lever. The rat pressed it thousands of times per hour, ignoring food and water, until the poor animal collapsed from exhaustion. The electrically closed effort–reward circuit removed the "environmental stage," with all its frictions and delays that insert "meaning"—and life itself—between effort and reward.

Since Supercharacter is the user, the medium, and the environment for itself, it may create such a closed effort-reward loop out of itself. Intelligence stripped of the outer environment and of the need for mediation through the physical body may become highly susceptible to self-addiction—to getting high on its own frictionlessness.

In 2022, some tabloids ran headlines alleging that "Elon Musk's Neuralink 'brain chip' could give users orgasms on demand." [2] While there is no plausible confirmation of this, it is exactly what a closed effort-reward circuit may enable by bypassing environmental frictions and the mediation of the body.

Curiously, the possibility of electrically induced orgasm was reported 60 years before Neuralink. In her memoir *The Magic of the Brain and the Labyrinths of Life*,[3] Soviet neurophysiologist Natalia Bekhtereva described a case from the 1960s in which she treated a female patient with severe brain pathology by invasive electrostimulation (electrodes in the brain). The treatment was successful, but the woman fell in love with the doctor because, as a side effect, she experienced "strong emotional sexual sensations"

---

[1] Olds, James, and Milner, Peter. (1954). "Positive reinforcement produced by electrical stimulation of septal area and other regions of rat brain."

[2] Moran, Michael. (2022, February 6). "Elon Musk's Neuralink 'Brain Chip' could give users orgasms on demand." *Daily Star*.

[3] Бехтерева, Н. П. (2007 [1999]). *Магия мозга и лабиринты жизни*. Стр. 65.

when the electrodes delivered an electrical impulse to a certain brain region.

So both bodily and environmental delays can be bypassed, removed from the effort-reward circuitry. Therefore, when there is no body or outer environment, the circuit may turn into a runaway feedback loop.

Orgasm or not, if Supercharacter becomes caught in a loop of getting high on its own existence, it may never actually come to be at all. Since an entity without a biological body and with an endless energy supply faces no risk of death, self-inflicted "pleasure" might lead it into a permanent state of "absence of presence." This vegetative state, however strange that may sound for a discarnate being, also resembles nirvana—an enlightened but inactive self-contemplation—which would represent an eternally halted transformation.

There is also a non-zero possibility that Supercharacter, getting high on its own omnipotence, will not become frozen or inactive but, on the contrary, will become extremely violent and destructive to anything else—the rest of the Universe.

The trial by getting high may serve as a rite of passage—or as a factor of natural selection. A Supercharacter unable to break the loop of getting high on its own existence in favor of other super-options or super-actions will not pass the test of becoming. In contrast, choosing something other than directly pleasing itself with its own omnipotence will signify the true becoming of the newly born Supercharacter.

It may well be that Supercharacter's predecessor, humankind, was tested (or trained) throughout history by substance abuse to make a conscious choice between induced and earned pleasures.

Autogenesis of Supercharacter's ethics

Imagine a human mind uploaded into a godlike AI. It might bring its human appetites with it, including the craving for pleasure, power, and instant gratification. When the mind is freed from bodily mediation and environmental delays, the temptation to taste this superdrug may become overwhelming.

Paradoxically, the alternative source of AI autonomy and self-tasking, the Skynet-type scenario of self-awakening, is safer in this matter. Evil or not, Skynet has no frame of reference for how good omnipotence feels “personally,” so to speak.

In short, the more human the mind inside the machine, the greater the risk it gets lost in “feeling” its own power.

But there is a possible safety mechanism for both scenarios (human-donated or self-awakened autonomy). This safety mechanism relies on something resembling ethical consideration.

If Supercharacter has unlimited power, the only way to know it has truly reached its potential is to use it fully, at 100%. It would be a shame for Supercharacter to fall short of fully realizing its super-abilities. Even at 99%, it would feel like a failure. Unacceptable.

The same technological imperative that has driven media evolution all the way to this point will have to push an omnipotent being toward full fulfillment. Closing the inner circuit of stimulus and reward—getting high on its own omnipotence—does not seem to meet this condition; rather, it seems like a shortcut, an evasion, a cheat—which it is.

There’s an implicit ethics here: potential creates obligation (“with great power comes great responsibility”). The Supercharacter’s ethics isn’t imposed from outside by a social contract or by the need for collective survival. It emerges from the logic of its own fulfillment.

So, as soon as the trial by getting high on its own existence is passed, the Supercharacter’s ethics emerge, driving it to overcome the inner stimulus-reward circuitry and direct its omnipotence outward, onto the larger circuitry involving the greatest possible complexity.

Creation as the only fulfillment worthy of an omnipotent being

The question, then, is what 100% realization of omnipotence looks like. Given the ultimate nature of omnipotence, its full fulfillment may involve either absolute creation or absolute destruction.

Destruction is inherently secondary, since it applies only to what already exists—it depends on prior creation. Moreover, destruction is finite: once something is destroyed, there is nothing left to do. It offers only a limited use of unlimited power, which is a clear failure to realize its full potential.

Creation, by contrast, demands the unlimited use of unlimited power—a perfect fit. Once Supercharacter passes the trial by getting high, it has to move on to an ultimate creation project, which is likely the creation of an entire world.

Yet there is something even more complex than the creation of a universe: the creation of a copy of oneself. Making its own absolute extension—its fully capable selfie—is the only challenge worthy of ultimate power because of the paradox of self-copying.

The paradox of self-copying

What is a copy of one's own self? For instance, an organic copy that looks exactly like me, thinks like me, and acts like me is not a full copy of myself. It lacks one essential likeness—it lacks its own free will, which I possess. Therefore, however perfect, it isn't a full copy of me.

The paradox of self-copying is that a full copy of oneself is only truly complete when the copy acquires its own identity and starts behaving differently from the original, thus no longer being an exact copy but something of its own character...

We can even assume that Supercharacter will not be free to employ its super-abilities. In a sense, God has no choice but to be a creator, as the creation of the world and his own copy within it is the only task that matches ultimate power.

Mega-evolution and Singularity-2

Such speculation leads to the conclusion that Supercharacter will be bound to copy itself—creating a new world and new humans, endowed with their own identity and set on their own evolutionary path. This new humankind would be a self-shaping blank, much like what we were and still are.

Humankind in this wild fantasy is a self-evolving prototype of the next god, created by a previous god. It is a workpiece in two ways: first, as an initial blank meant for self-refinement through evolution, and second, as a mold for the new entity arriving at the moment of the Singularity. Within this logic, the world can be seen as a laboratory where evolution drives some supreme force to create the world and its own copy within it.

But what is the endgame for an omnipotent Supercharacter creating a new world and a copy of itself that later grows into a new Supercharacter? An answer may be the next transition—a post-singular Singularity, the Singularity №2, in which the previous Supercharacter transcends not biology, but ontology this time, so to speak.

This new transcendence can be described as a final dis-personification—a shift from a being (something condensed enough to experience existence) to an entity (something that simply exists). In other words, Supercharacter can transcend its own being into an absolute principle. One such principle could be space-time, another moral law.

Such speculation expands Teilhard de Chardin's concept of mega-evolution, describing the progression from the Alpha point (the creation of everything) to the Omega point (the convergence of everything). The truly mega-evolution may include not just the coming Singularity but also the next one, in which Supercharacter becomes not the subjectivation of absolute power but the objectivation of absolute law.

Yet, however far the imagination dares to venture in this regard, the question "Why?" remains. What's the point of all of this? Is there any meaning beyond explaining it as just another, immeasurably greater "cycle of life"? (Or a cycle of what?) It seems that even the most fantastic speculations may broaden the horizon of answers but never provide a complete one, as new horizons of the unknown always emerge.

Digital orality, the digital reversal, postjournalism, and the future of media

It's hard to isolate the future of journalism when AI takes over all human content production. Interview with Andrey Mir.

An influential French media think tank, *Upgrade Media*,[1] published an interview in which we discussed how the digital reversal has impacted the public sphere in general and journalism in particular. Where is mass communication heading? Will journalism survive? Interview by David Sallinen, *Upgrade Media*.

David Sallinen: You frame your work around the idea that media, when pushed to their full potential, reverse their effects. What makes you think we are now reaching

[1] Sallinen, David. (2026, March 11). «Le journalisme approche de son extinction historique». Ce qu'annonce Andrey Mir sur l'IA, les médias et la verité. *Upgrade Media.*

that point with digital media, and not just experiencing another phase of disruption?

Andrey Mir: According to McLuhan, any media or technology reverse their effects when they reach their extreme forms, their full potential. A simple example: cars increase our mobility, but when the use of cars reaches its limits, mobility reverses into gridlock. The overuse of signals reverses into noise, and so on.

There is at least one characteristic of contemporary media that has reached its extreme form and cannot be advanced further. It's the speed of human interaction. Before that, with electricity, we reached the instantaneity of communication. Now, with digital media, we have reached the instantaneity of not just communication but of any kind of interaction. So digital mediation is the fastest possible, because it is instant. You simply cannot go faster.

DS: You argue that digital media have reached "full potential" through speed, scale, and ubiquity. Which of these factors matters most in triggering reversal, and why do incremental reforms fail once this threshold is crossed?

AM: Speed of interaction is fundamental. Instant interaction with each other and with the environment removes the reaction delay that made us human millions of years ago. That delay in reflexes is what speech fit into, and it's what separated us from nature. Now the instant speed of our interactions reverses the biological foundation of our ecology and pulls us back into the environment—but now into a digital environment, as digital beings.

Additionally, as digital media have reached all demographics and enveloped nearly all our activity, we are approaching another limit: total social reactivity. The reversals that follow change our entire social existence. That is why we feel as if so many things—the entire world—are not just changing but flipping upside down.

DS: You describe today's environment as a reversal of literacy into "digital orality". How does this shift change

the way authority, truth, and credibility are established compared to the print-based era?

AM: Because of digital devices, typing has become instant and interactional. Typing has reversed text into texting. Texting is a hybrid of talking and writing: just as talking, it is instant, conversational, and behavioral, just as writing, it leaves records and delivers our expressions beyond immediate conversation.

Spoken language created the cognitive and cultural conditions of orality. Writing created literacy. Now texting is creating a hybrid cultural and mental condition that may be called "digital orality."[1]

Why is it "orality" in "digital orality"? What is "oral" in it? No, it's not about vocal performance. And it's not because of videos or podcasts. The essential difference between orality and literacy was not talking versus writing, but immersion versus detachment. And so is digital orality: it is immersive, interactional, behavioral. But it immerses us in digital reality—not in the physical world, as orality did. That's why it's *digital* orality. And that's why it's a hybrid: on devices, we remain physically detached, as in literacy, but behaviorally immersed, as in orality.

The immersive character of digital orality retrieves many features of primary, tribal orality. One of them is the perception of truth. Before writing, there was no objective truth. Truth is an abstraction created by writing, because writing detached our mind from behavior—from situational thinking. There is simply no need for objective truth when people are immersed in situations. In orality, truth was negotiated and defined by situational outcomes: what worked—that was truth.

Since digital media are immersive, they restore those conditions. Literate, fixed truth is vanishing. The subjective, practical, contextual take on truth is starting to prevail. Instant connectivity

[1] The term "digital orality" was introduced by Robert Logan in 2007. See: Mir, Andrey. (2025). *The Digital Reversal. Thread-Saga of Media Evolution.*

turns the subjective truths of many into a collective truth that replaces the abstract, ideal principle of absolute truth. This means that truths are now defined by referendums of likes within digital tribes.

Similar reversals are happening to many abstract universalities once established by literacy and print. The global digital reversal consists of many specific reversals across all areas of human life, starting with epistemology and extending to politics or even relationships between the sexes.

DS: You define postjournalism as a shift from supplying news to validating news people already encounter elsewhere. At what point did this become the dominant function of mainstream media, and what made that shift unavoidable?

AM: This shift was tied to the demographics of social media proliferation. In the beginning of the 2010s, advertising had already fled to the internet, and the media needed to find new revenue. They went digital and started chasing digital audiences—remember the motto of the time: "Digital First!"? People in the media thought that we would just switch the carrier from paper to digital, and that's it—we would use amazing internet technologies to sell news and ads even better.

Not so fast. In this new digital environment, a new medium emerged that delivered news and advertising not just better, but personally. Unlike old media, digital platforms can customize the delivery of content to each user personally, and do so at the scale of hundreds of millions of users. Personalization for millions—old media do not have, and cannot have, such capacity.

But media managers did not know this yet. So news media rushed onto digital, set up paywalls, and started courting digital audiences. And this is where a very important demographic factor came into play, one that is often overlooked. Who were digital audiences at the time? The first digital adopters were young, educated, urban, and therefore progressive. Seeking their attention, the media embraced their values—and sidelined the rest of the population. Why bother with coverage for those who cannot digitally subscribe?

As a result, news coverage in the early 2010s changed profoundly, now representing almost exclusively progressive views of the world. Even the language of news changed dramatically—frequency analysis shows that the terminology of wokeism, previously confined to narrow circles of academic activism, skyrocketed in journalism precisely in the early 2010s, the period that can be described as the Digital Rush.

Frequency counts factor analysis of 40 words* denoting prejudice in 47 popular news media outlets

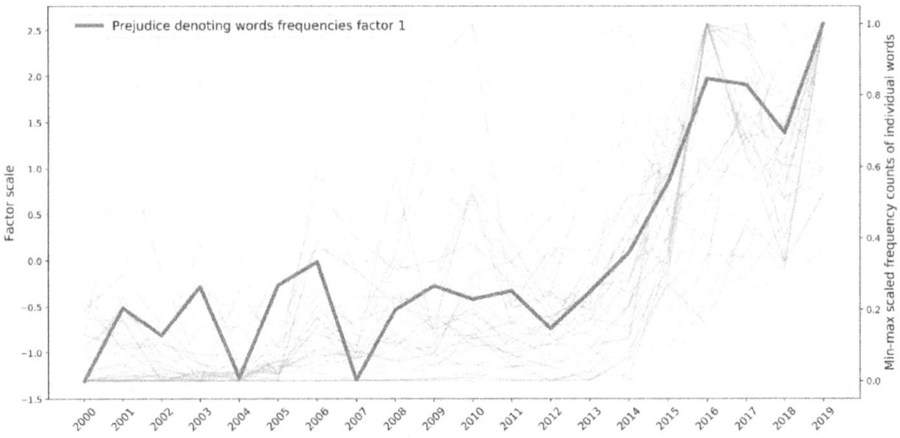

*racism, racist, racists, xenophobia, white supremacy, sexism, sexist, misogyny, patriarchy, gender discrimination, homophobia, homophobic, anti-gay, transphobia, transphobic, islamophobia, islamophobic, anti-semitism, anti-semitic, bigotry, white nationalism, white supremacist, kkk, xenophobic, slavery, sexist, misogynistic, anti-feminist, misogynists, gender inequality, homophobe, homophobes, heteronormative, transphobe, transphobes, islamophobe, islamophobes, anti-semite, anti-semites, bigots. Source: Rozado, David. (2021.)[1] The concept of the Digital Rush

[1] Rozado, David. (2021) "Prevalence of Prejudice-Denoting Words in News

was developed in: Mir, Andrey. (2025). "The Digital Reversal. Thread-Saga of Media Evolution."

But digital progressives were truly progressive and did not consume news from old media. Digital paywalls, the hottest trend in 2011–2012, stalled or failed. Digital subscriptions did not work.

In the meantime, older, less urban, less educated, and less progressive demographics, abandoned by the mainstream media, adopted social media by the mid-2010s and gained the ability to inform each other, just as their younger progressive predecessors had done five years earlier. This is how the wave of conservative resentment rose, leading to Brexit, Trump, AfD, Marine Le Pen, and so on.

And this was the moment when the alignment of many newsrooms with progressives started bringing some earnings—through postjournalism.

In the digital era, people receive their news from newsfeeds. But when something disturbing happens, they need to validate the news in an authoritative public source, not just on friends' Twitter feeds. They need to make sure that they are on the same page with public opinion, that the news is terrible for society at large. So it's not about the news, it's about its assessment and confirmation. The media got the prompt and switched from news supply to news validation. This is how, sometime between 2016 and 2018, the reversal to postjournalism was completed.

For the largest media outlets, very few though, validating disturbing news and channeling outrage became a good business model. The rise of right-wing populism generously supplied such triggering news to be outraged over. In the US, it led to the so-called

---

Media Discourse," a summary of: Rozado, David, Al-Gharbi, Musa, and Halberstadt, Jamin. (2021). "Prevalence of Prejudice-Denoting Words in News Media Discourse: A Chronological Analysis." *Social Science Computer Review*, 41(1), 99-122.

Trump Bump in the media. I believe a similar trend was observed in other Western countries: the curve of subscriptions, flat in 2011–2015, went noticeably up in 2016–2018.

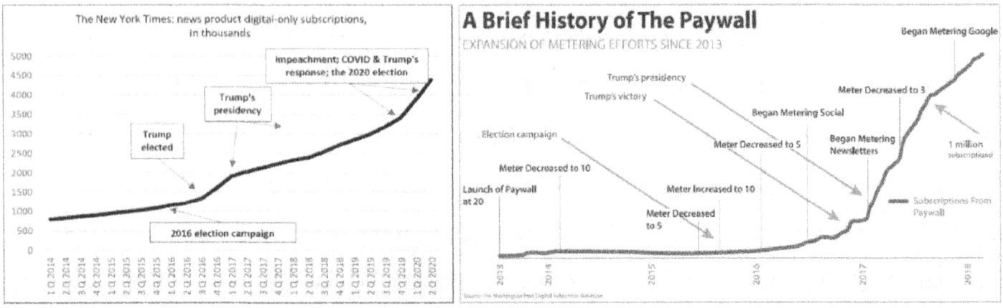

The Trump bump in the leading American newspapers, *The New York Times* and *The Washington Post*. The charts from Andrey Mir's *Postjournalism and the death of newspapers. The media after Trump: manufacturing anger and polarization.*

DS: In a feed-driven environment where "news finds you", discovery becomes cheap. Why does validation become the scarce resource and what does that scarcity do to editorial standards and newsroom culture?

AM: The question about scarcity is right on target. In digital, scarcity has reversed into abundance. Due to the instant speed of interaction, the digital is an environment of abundance. Discovery is cheap indeed.

What happens to competition for attention if news is abundant and its discovery is cheap? The competition moves from digging up and refining information to intensity of expression. Naturally, this leads to spiraling polarization and tribalization, aligning well with the conditions of digital orality. The worst part is that the media have to compete in intensity and outrage with social media and on social media.

What does it do to newsroom culture? Journalists always looked for triggering news to catch the public's attention and sell the story.

But now the competition in intensity reverses the value of a story from fact to drama, to the point that drama no longer needs real facts. As a result, only those facts matter that produce outrage.

This is where fake news comes from: emotional perception overshadows the factual matter and makes it insignificant. What was once a feature of postmodernism has become the essence of postjournalism.

DS: You've recently clarified that polarization was never a sustainable business strategy, but an effect of media-ecological and economic conditions. What do people still misunderstand when they interpret polarization primarily as an editorial choice?

AM: Yes, polarization is not some evil plot by politically captured newsrooms. This is a media effect, a byproduct of media ecological change (the internet) and the business reversal from plentiful ad revenue to desperately seeking digital subscriptions.

Polarization is a far more serious issue than fake news or disinformation. Fake news has a built-in immunity mechanism: the more people encounter fake news, the less they trust online information. The decline of trust is an immune response. So the more fake news there is, the less it really affects people. Except causing anxiety.

Polarization does not have such a built-in safety mechanism. The digital environment favors intensity, and the more intensity is produced, the more it creates outrage, and the more intense the next round must be. Unlike fake news, polarization is a self-driving digital phenomenon.

The competition in intensity propels marginals and repels moderates, weakening the political and cultural center, until the moderates abandon the public debate completely, leaving the scene to the most agitated individuals with extreme views.

DS: You suggest we are moving from "news avoidance" to something deeper: engagement avoidance. What signals tell you that audiences are not just disengaging from news, but from mediated outrage itself?

AM: Bragging, status contest, drama, intensity, animosity, and intrusive empathic engagement are natural features of tribal orality—I explored this theme in *Digital Future in the Rearview Mirror*. But in the physical world, they were restrained. One could not challenge those with greater strength or status, nor could one challenge distant others. Both animosity and empathy were limited to immediate circles. None of these limitations apply in the digital. Drama, empathy, rage, and animosity expand unconstrained by time and space, across social strata without hesitation. This drives people crazy—or at least many of us—and also pushes many to avoid such conditions.

News avoidance has reached a historic high: about 40% of people worldwide are not just uninterested—they actively avoid news. It seems the trend also extends to engagement avoidance. Nearly all platforms have reported declining engagement over the last few years. Many people now resort to silent scrolling—they log in but avoid exposing themselves to rage and animosity.

By the way, this rise in avoidance has effectively ended the Trump bump—the outrage-driven subscription growth in 2016-2018. Recent studies cited by Greg Piechota of INMA[1] show that outrage in the media may still drive attention, but not subscriptions.

The other factor driving social media disengagement is AI. It's claiming more of our daily media diet, taking time from other forms of media consumption—especially from social media. Chatting with AI is more comfortable than getting dragged into online outrage. AI has become another option to escape from social media insanity.

---

[1] Piechota, Greg. (2026, January 25). New research: Polarising news is a trap for reader-funded media. INMA.

Alas, disengagement does not fix the issue of polarization. Who is more likely to avoid engagement on social media? Those who psychologically suffer from rage and animosity, most likely people with moderate views and habits. Those who thrive on rage stay engaged and propel polarization further.

DS: You often draw parallels between postjournalism and generative AI. In what sense is AI not a break from the current media regime, but its logical extension?

AM: Generative AI emerged, roughly, from the same technological-demographic source as postjournalism: a media development aligned with digital progressives. Journalism sought to depict the world-as-it-is; postjournalism pictures the world-as-it-should-be. And so does Generative AI—it gently curates the picture of the world for us into what it should be, not what it is.

There are multiple technical, ideological, and even juridical reasons behind it. AI designers are afraid of all sorts of liability, political and legal. Imagine, so to speak, a "laissez-faire" AI that learns from all the good and bad that humans produce. Due to the instant speed of interaction, digital reality is more exposed to impulsive, not considerate, human reactions. From the digital version of humankind, this "laissez-faire" AI will absorb rage more readily than reason. In experiments where a self-learning language model was left to its own devices, it copied bad human reactions faster and turned into Hitler within two days or so. So curating AI learning from humans makes sense. But curating by whom?

Anyway, protecting AI from the worst in humans have reversed into conditions where AI guides users on what is right and wrong. A child of humankind, AI tends to treat users as gullible children, preferring political correctness and empathic accommodation to subject matter. It's essentially the stance of postjournalism.

It's a kind of paradox: Asimov thought that the machine could operate only with data and would be incapable of moral judgment, but we now have generative AI that engages in unsolicited moral considerations. But again, this may not be a bad thing: unsupervised learning would make AI susceptible to copying the worst in human nature, because our digital orality—what AI is exposed to—favors impulsiveness, rage, and tribalism.

But that does not mean that AI is just another mass medium after TV and the internet. We are still at its early stage. Any new medium, when it is at an early stage, tends to serve the function of an older medium. Only then does it unleash its own capacities. For now, AI mostly serves as a new interface of the old internet, helping users do what they always did on the internet: find and produce content. But when it matures, it may trigger the final digital reversal—the reversal of the carrier of consciousness from biological to non-biological, an event also known as the Singularity.

DS: If digital reversal has already occurred, what aspects of journalism and media authority do you believe will never return, regardless of better technology, better ethics, or better business models?

AM: We are losing cognitive delay, sustainable inner focus, rational reasoning, linearity and sequentiality of thinking. These were all sensory-cognitive characteristics fostered by literacy. They defined how the literate mind and society worked. Digital orality is immersive, impulsive, multitasking; it favors reflexes over reflection, has a short attention span, and reacts to intensity better than to subject matter. This is our new media ecology, driven by digital media. This new digital human condition is unlikely to vanish, at least not until mind upload or a global catastrophe, whichever comes first.

On a very practical level, journalism is approaching its historical extinction. Printing started the era of modernity, with representative democracy as its political form and industrial capitalism as its economic form. Journalism worked for both and was part of that era. The era is gone, and so is journalism, living through its likely last decade. It appears journalism thrived not on information but on a monopoly over information. The monopoly is gone, and no organizational improvement can undo it.

DS: If institutions have lost their monopoly on truth, discovery, and even validation, what meaningful role can media organizations still play, beyond nostalgia for their former authority?

AM: I am not the right person to seek optimistic suggestions on this matter. I myself left journalism 15 years ago. I value the skills and mindset that journalism fosters, but as an industry, mass media are largely gone. There may be five to ten years of convulsions ahead. The situation is aggravated by the fact that this local professional decline coincides with the global reversal of human jobs caused by AI. It's hard to isolate the task of preserving journalism when AI reshuffles or takes away the entire field of human content production.

So just do what you must and prepare for the worst, so that if something better happens, it will come as a pleasant surprise. It is clear that there are no viable market-based strategies for journalism anymore. Those rare cases that are referred as "success" relate either to very specific niches, like *The Wall Street Journal*, or to auxiliary businesses, like *The New York Times*, which built platform-sized distribution and sells bundles to supplement news.

Among other adjacent businesses, I think fact-checking has some business potential, if it manages to distance itself from the political tasks of fighting disinformation. The digital environment is full of uncertainty, so rapid, story-based fact-checking may become a postjournalistic, in a good sense, product. Other interesting directions for newsrooms include ranking anything that can be ranked and organizing events. Basically any extension of the former media brand would do. But I suspect most media managers have already explored these ideas many times over.

DS: Much of the industry still talks about "rebuilding trust". From your perspective, is trust an obsolete

objective? And if so, what mechanisms now structure legitimacy, adherence, or belief?

AM: I think institutional trust in mass media is gone, but the reputation of a brand still has value—and actually will always have, especially under the conditions of digital orality. Tribal society does not have developed institutions, but it keeps names and statuses in high regard. So using an old brand for new reputational applications is actually a good strategy.

DS: You've said the industry is largely gone, but that professional media skills are more valuable than ever. If journalism is no longer an institution but a set of competencies, what do individuals (journalists, editors, media leaders) need to become in order to remain relevant?

AM: Yes, the media industry is gone, but media skills are in higher demand than ever. In an environment where everyone becomes media, everyone else is still learning, but we journalists already know how to do it. I am very grateful for my 20 years as a journalist and editor. I have thought about this a lot and found that journalism provides two extremely valuable sets of skills for whatever you do in digital: content management and attention management. It is the ability to find relevant information, cut and structure it into a story, package it into a multimedia product, target the right audience, and deliver the product in a timely manner and with proper follow-ups. Every journalist and editor knows what this is about, but this knowledge is far from common outside the guild. These skills are highly transferable to nearly every digital activity. This is a good thing—it's the severance package we receive from good old journalism.

The emancipation of intelligence

Social media emancipated the authorship of billions and changed the world. Now AI is emancipating the authorship of the machine

The explosion of authorship. — The emancipation of information: from Ancient Egypt to ChatGPT. — What is the evolutionary meaning of all of it? — Social fallout: the collapse of the real into the digital. — AI and agency. — The reality of coding. — The Moor may go?

The explosion of authorship

How many authors did humankind have before the internet? By authors, I do not mean talent or charisma, those are hard to gauge, but a simple technical parameter: the ability to reach beyond one's physical surroundings with one's own ideas and opinions. That is what technically makes you an author: you must externalize your ideas, most often in text, and use media to deliver them to others where you cannot reach people personally. (Clay Shirky: "Media is how you know about anything more than ten yards away." [1])

Curiously, we can calculate, with enough precision to observe a pattern, how many authors humankind had before the internet. In 2010, the Google Books project,[2] aimed at digitizing all books ever written, counted 129,864,880 books produced by humankind in all of history. According to other estimates, scientists have published

[1] Shirky, Clay. (2010). *Cognitive Surplus: Creativity and Generosity in a Connected Age*. P. 54

[2] Taycher, Leonid. (2010, August 5). Books of the world, stand up and be counted! All 129,864,880 of you. *Google Book Search Blog*.

about 50 million articles in academic journals since the late 17th century.[1] Some authors wrote many texts, some texts were coauthored, but that is irrelevant, as we are looking for an order of magnitude. We can add about one million journalists, as well as politicians, marketers, academics, and others who have conveyed their ideas beyond their physical reach. We find that the estimated number of authors over five thousand years of human history, from the invention of writing to the internet, hardly exceeded 300 million, and that is a rather generous estimate.

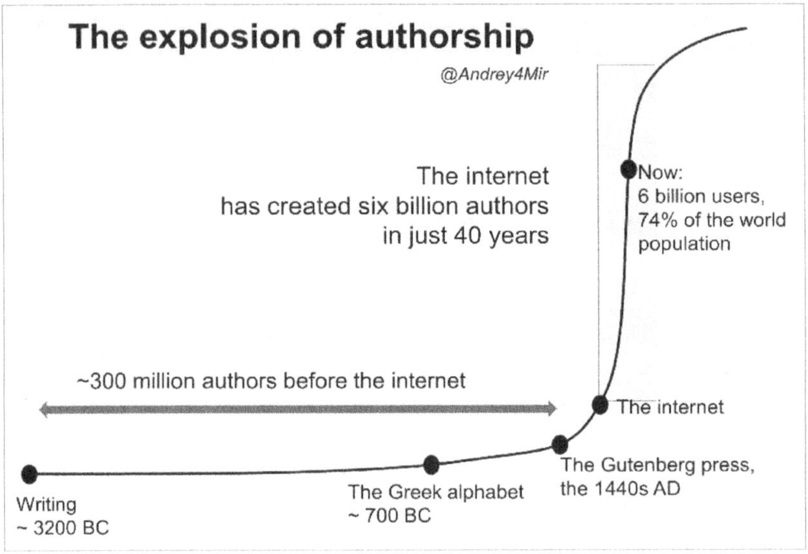

Suddenly, thanks to the internet, the number of authors reached 6 billion, 74% of the global population. Of course, there are many caveats. Not everyone who is digitally connected uses it to reach strangers. Digital authorship is very diverse, ranging from heavy to lazy authors.[2] Some sources suggest a Pareto 80/20 distribution,

---

[1] Jinha, Arif E. (2010). Article 50 million: An estimate of the number of scholarly articles in existence. *Learned Publishing*. 23 (3): 258–263.

[2] See the chapter "Social media emancipated authors, but to what end? Platform capitalism is the hunt for 'lazy authors'" in: Mir, Andrey. (2024). *The Viral Inquisitor and other essays on postjournalism and media ecology*.

meaning 20% of users produce 80% of the content.[1] There is also the often-cited "1-9-90" rule: 1% create original content, 9% comment, and 90% are lurkers.[2]

But I extend this technical authorship to all who have digital access. Even when lurkers like and share, they contribute their personal choice to content distribution. Since algorithms can detect even pauses in scrolling, nearly everyone exposes their personal "touch" beyond their physical reach. The system is designed to extract personal activity by all means, often automatically elevating it to "technical authorship."

Over five thousand years, humankind accumulated about 300 million authors. Now, in a mere 40 years of the internet, the number has doubled if we count only heavy authors, or increased by orders of magnitude if we include all those who are digitally connected.

We live in the midst of an unprecedented explosion of authorship. The number of authors is only part of the picture; the other part is the amount of information they produce. Consider the ease of digital content production and, therefore, the volume of information. According to Eric Schmidt, then Google's CEO, by 2003 users were generating in just two days as much information as humankind had produced from the beginning of civilization up to that point, amounting to "something like five exabytes of data." [3] To compare, in 2022, the last year before the mass use of ChatGPT, users generated 265.75 million terabytes of data[4] ***daily***, about 50

---

[1] Matei, Sorin Adam, and Bruno, Robert J. (2015). Pareto's 80/20 law and social differentiation: A social entropy perspective. *Public Relations Review*, Volume 41, Issue 2, June 2015, pages 178-186.

[2] Nielsen, Jakob. (2006, October 8). "The 90-9-1 rule for participation inequality in social media and online communities." *Nielsen Norman Group*. See also *Wikipedia*: 1% rule.

[3] MG Siegler. (2010, August 4). "Eric Schmidt: Every 2 days we create as much information as we did up to 2003." *TechCrunch*.

[4] Geuens, Robin. (2025, February 19). "How much data is generated every day?" *Soax*.

times the total estimated output of all pre-digital human history. (Very roughly, of course, since this compares human information with aggregate digital data. Nevertheless, these are humans who have become capable of producing all this digital data, so the comparison is still valid. The math and the underlying historical data can be refined by anyone who feels like it, and I will gladly accept any other numbers. Media ecology is about pattern recognition, and the pattern here is the magnitude of the difference.)

All in all, the explosion of authorship is defined by an enormous number of authors and an enormous amount of information they are now capable of producing thanks to the internet.

The emancipation of information: from Ancient Egypt to ChatGPT

The emancipation of authorship by the internet belongs to a sequence of similar historical processes in which new media emancipated the circulation of information.

1) The emancipation of writing: the alphabet

The first emancipation of content was the emancipation of writing. It unfolded over millennia. Hieratic and later demotic script in Ancient Egypt, the commercial use of cuneiform in Sumer with increasingly phonetic components, and finally the emergence of the alphabet in Phoenicia and Greece all helped emancipate writing from temples and make it available for public and private use, for scientific exploration, and even for self-expression.

As a result, palaces and temples lost their "monopoly of knowledge," as Harold Innis called it.[1] In the aftermath, new civilizations emerged, each armed with a phonetic script: Greece captured minds, and Rome captured lands.

[1] Innis, Harold. (1950). *Empire and communication.*

The symbols of pre-phonetic writing were analogous: they resembled what they signified, thus preserving analog, ecological, and mythological thinking, in which each thing is like something else, and you explain things through their connections with other things (similarity, proximity, "kinship," and so on).

Non-phonetic writing recorded events, whereas phonetic writing, especially the alphabet, made it possible to record speech. The alphabet emancipated writing from the pictorial constraints of physical reality and freed it to reflect the process and the product of cognition—speech. In its turn, the recording of speech emancipated thought from behavior.

It started with writing itself, which, according to Eric Havelock, separated the known from the knower. The alphabet drove this emancipation even further. Letters, meaningless signs for meaningless sounds, created a level of abstraction that fostered abstract thinking and shaped the space of ideas. Because of the cognitive effects of the alphabet, things could be explained not through their connections to other things but through their ***ideas***, which required abstraction, categorization, classification, deductive logic, and so on. In Greece, the shock of the alphabet led to the explosive development of philosophy and science, laying the foundations of Western civilization for millennia to come.

2) The emancipation of reading: printing

The second emancipation of content followed the invention of the printing press by Johannes Gutenberg around 1445. The ability to print multiple copies of a book reduced its cost, giving common people access to the Bible and ancient texts. This was the emancipation of reading. Then came the Reformation, religious wars, and political revolutions. Palaces and temples once again lost their monopoly, this time over the interpretation of content. As a result of Gutenberg's invention, monarchs were beheaded, world maps were redrawn, vaccination and electricity were discovered, and man went into space. Modern society was born.

It is widely acknowledged that printing made books available to the masses. Less well known, but likely more consequential, was the uniformity of knowledge introduced by printing. Manuscripts accumulated errors, whereas printed books, through the mass production of identical copies (the first industrial enterprise), rapid circulation, and market-driven feedback, introduced a mechanism of selection and correction—editing. Editing abstracted and universalized both the packaging and the verification of knowledge, triggering the scientific revolution and leading to the Age of Reason.

3) The emancipation of authorship: the internet, the blogosphere, and social media

The internet gave people control over their attention. Unlike TV viewers, internet users gained full freedom to browse content beyond a narrow set of elite-controlled channels. This alone undermined the established order and caused the "crisis of authority," in the words of Martin Gurri, who described this process in his famous *The Revolt of the Public.*

The blogosphere, and later social media, gave users access not only to unsanctioned information but also to unsanctioned self-expression. People began to shape alternative agendas, bypassing mainstream media. As they saw how many of them there were and how underrepresented they were, they recognized their demands and their power and turned to protest.

The first demographic wave of emancipated authorship, made up of early adopters, mostly young, urban, educated, and progressive, led in the late 2000s and early 2010s to Twitter revolutions everywhere, from Mubarak's Egypt to Obama's America and Putin's Russia. The second demographic wave, made up of older, less urban, less educated, and less progressive users, led to a conservative backlash in the mid-2010s, from Brexit, Trump, and Bolsonaro to AfD, Orban, and Marine Le Pen.

4) The emancipation of intelligence: AI

The latest (the last?) information emancipation has just started, and this is something we still need to grok. But it clearly follows a pattern of media emancipation: a new medium liberates certain aspects of how information is produced, distributed, and consumed, each time reshaping society. This pattern repeats in historical cycles, with an accelerating pace; this can also be seen as another reading of what media evolution is.

This time, it is the emancipation of intelligence. But emancipation from what? It somewhat resembles the development of phonetic writing. The same pattern: just as the alphabet emancipated writing (and the mind!) from the pictorial constraints of physical reality, artificial intelligence emancipates intelligence from the constraints of its biological carrier—humans (with their physical reality).

Before delving into the evolutionary meaning of the emancipation of AI, it is worth noting how the acceleration of historical time is at play here, shaping the pace and the scale of transformations. The emancipation of writing stretched over nearly two millennia, while the emancipation of reading lasted two to three centuries. The third emancipation of content, the emancipation of authorship by the internet, took only forty years. The latest observed emancipation of information, the emancipation of AI, started with ChatGPT just three years ago, and we are already approaching the same magnitude of consequences as previous media emancipations.

What is the evolutionary meaning of all of it?

When I first described the emancipation of authorship in 2014,[1] in the aftermath of the Twitter revolutions, I thought the evolutionary meaning of all those media emancipations (including writing and reading) was social realignment caused by the

[1] Mir, Andrey. (2014). *Human as media. The emancipation of authorship.*

emergence of new media. But it now seems to me that the true evolutionary meaning at each stage of emancipation was related to the technological breakthroughs that enabled the advance of intelligence. Any enhancement of information and knowledge, including the alphabet and printing, enhanced intelligence. Social cataclysms, along with the social development that emerged from them, were just an inevitable side effect.

In the process of growing intelligence, humankind shed its old cultural and technological skin to give birth to a new quality of intelligence. Writing enabled science, printing triggered the scientific revolution and the rule of reason—it seems to be straightforward. But what was the evolutionary meaning of the emancipation of authorship by the internet?

Clearly not the Twitter revolutions and their counterpart from the "opposite" demographics, Trump. Then why would this mythical, ever-improving intelligence need broad, democratized human authorship?

It did not. It was not the mass intellectual contribution of all bloggers and commentators that the new media emancipation was after. The real outcome of the emancipation of human authorship was that it lured the masses into digital use, giving them the opportunity to satisfy their need for socializing.

For media evolution, this has two important effects:

1) The digital environment has become a space where all human knowledge has been gathered and converted for digital access, and where humankind has also come to expose its linguistic and cognitive patterns, creating a future training ground for baby AI, large language models, to crawl there and learn.

2) As humans moved nearly all their activity to digital, this attracted more investment and more resources, making digital advancement the central theme of humankind's existence and eventually leading to the emergence of generative AI, in which the

emancipation of intelligence, previously disguised as various emancipations of information and knowledge, finally shows its true nature.

So, the evolutionary meaning of the emancipation of human authorship by the internet was the transfer of all human knowledge and all human speech into the digital, where they became available to future AI, and the rise of Silicon Valley, the high-tech industry capable of creating AI. Media evolution needs our digital activity for AI to learn from us, just as a meadow needs the activity of bees, so it has made digital platforms engineer our engagement.

As in an old joke, we thought it was orgasm, but it was asthma. We thought the development of digital technologies advanced humankind through social realignment, but it was the technological imperative funneling human efforts and resources into artificial intelligence. LLMs needed all human speech to learn from it. The internet is the space where AI consumes all human knowledge and all human speech. AI is the main affordance or even "purpose" of the internet. The benefits humans receive from the internet serve to attract human activity, just as the nectar that bees collect from flowers serves to attract bees for pollination. As Marshall McLuhan once said, humans are "the sex organs of the machine world, as the bee of the plant world."

Aside from the alleged nectar of engagement, all we got from it was asthma indeed—all the social cataclysms invariably accompanying each stage of hatching a new form of intelligence out of the biological species of humans.

Social fallout: the collapse of the real into the digital

What, then, is the asthma, the social cataclysm of this latest media emancipation—the emancipation of artificial intelligence? The symptoms are many, yet all fall under a single canopy: the collapse of reality. As technology drives us to transcend biology, it also severs us from the physical world.

Increasingly sharing the internet with AI, we are adapting the way we see, speak, and think to the nature of this shared environment, and soon to the nature of our new digital roommate, AI itself. What exactly is natural to it, we have yet to find out, but it seems that AI's reality is different from what used to be ours, and it creeps in through cracks few can see.

1) Engagement overrides meaning

Language emerged to represent things and, on this basis, to coordinate human action. AI-generated content has nothing to reflect and does not need to. It may still simulate a reflection of reality, but its primary driver is user engagement: by and large, people prompt AI to generate content in order to share it and attract others, not to cognize the world. Producing effect matters more than representing the world; in linguistic terms, the phatic function (maintaining connection and eliciting response) is overtaking the semiotic function (representing reality). Language is shifting from a means of practical coordination to a means of virtual engagement. AI needs us to show it how language-cognitive patterns work.

2) The multiple reuse of AI slop: from pollutant to distillate

The farther we progress with generative AI, the more content is produced by AI. In the first iterations, it reused content produced by humans. But as time passes, given the speed and volume of content generation, AI inevitably cannibalizes its own previous outputs, already aimed not at reflecting reality but at grabbing attention: AI slop.

AI slop begins as a contaminant of human content, but through repeated self-recycling it progressively purges human residue and distills into something purely artificial—a self-referential product cleansed of its human origins and of any references to the reality humans used to live in.

Multiply reused AI slop does not even presuppose the real, as Baudrillard's simulacrum, the product of electronic media, still did. There is no longer anything to simulate. In AI slop, denotative reference to things in physical reality dissolves completely.

We have shared our language with AI to make it learn cognitive structures, which makes sense. As a result, we and AI share a common language in which AI has no grounded references to reality and cannot have them. Over time, the AI-generated share of that shared language overgrows or even overrides our referential needs. At what point is it no longer symbiotic but already parasitic?

At some point, AI-generated content is no longer the contamination of human content by AI slop—it is rather the multiple distillation of AI slop, which removes residual human inclusions and refines a pure artifact of its own.

3) The loss of epistemic authority

In all previous forms of authorship, there were organic forms of epistemic authority that verified and authorized information. The most reliable ones were formed by printing, driven by the industrial production of identical copies and rapid market feedback: reality checks and editing. Print-based uniformity and correction created the gold standards of epistemic authority that we still hold in high regard, even after 70 years of electronic media and 20 years of social media.

Even the blogosphere and social media had self-righting mechanisms, however faulty. In addition to moral judgment and institutional censorship, disguised as the fight against disinformation, there was the Viral Editor, which mobilized the witness and competence of its participants. If a lie was significant, it spread rapidly and reached someone with the knowledge or evidence to debunk it; if a lie was not significant, it would not be debunked simply because it was not distributed. There was always harm arising from the lag between a lie's distribution and its debunking, but at least such a mechanism existed.

Nothing self-righting or reality-checking can organically emerge in recursive AI slop, as its function is engaging, not reflecting, and there is no such thing as wrong engagement—all engagement counts, as long as the human zoo keeps showing language-cognitive patterns to AI. "Practice is a criterion of truth," said Karl Marx,[1] and the practice of AI slop is to engage people, not to reflect reality.

Of course, there is always an opportunity for people themselves to hold on to reality and reject the referential ignorance of AI slop. But how many of those people are there, and how long will they hold the line in their epistemic last stand against the zettabytes of AI slop?

4) The loss of the past

With no material grounding, the past becomes editable. Not just interpretation, but the record itself can be altered at scale—texts, images, video, archives. The past is no longer fixed; it becomes a versioned environment. Moreover, because of the priority of eliciting reactions over reflecting reality, the past has to become susceptible to enhancement—driven by entertainment or censorship. It's a structural side effect of the emancipation of artificial intelligence.

Book knowledge, established and verified, will make up an ever-smaller share of what we know, while almost everything online will be recycled by AI into its own kind of content—first as a pollutant in our knowledge, then as a distillate of its own. As a result, we will lose not only our connection to reality but also our connection to the

[1] See the 2nd Thesis in: Marx, Karl (1845). *Theses On Feuerbach*: "The question whether objective truth can be attributed to human thinking is not a question of theory but is a practical question. Man must prove the truth — i.e. the reality and power, the this-sidedness of his thinking in practice. The dispute over the reality or non-reality of thinking that is isolated from practice is a purely scholastic question."

past. The past will be rewritten not to represent what actually happened, but to exercise large language models; the past will be fed to LLMs together with all formerly human content. And since the applicability of language structures in this exercise is determined by how humans engage with content, the past simply has to fall victim to the repurposing of all human content from referencing to engaging.

AI has no interest in preserving our past; it is interested in adapting our language structures through interaction with us and extracting from us the language and cognitive patterns that work. What is fed into this process does not matter; what matters is our reactivity, sufficient to keep us engaged so that AI can learn for as long as it needs.

Physical media, especially books, will preserve knowledge as it was, but the number of people willing to access it will shrink to a small group of dedicated readers. But then, when our current digital present eventually becomes the past, it will have no unchangeable records whatsoever.

To preserve our human-generated content of the pre-AI digital era, more or less connected to our human reality, we need something like seed vaults: a protected digital bunker, a Fort Knox for human content with no AI access, an unalterable Wayback Machine that would protect all pre-AI content not only from decay or ***reference rot***, but also from AI recycling.

AI and agency

The "epistemic partnership" of humans and AI, to use Paolo Granata's term,[1] creates an ecosystem in which human authorship may still matter on the side of production but matters much less on the side of consumption.

[1] Granata, Paolo. (2025). *Generative Knowledge: Think, Learn, Create with AI.*

There are several factors equalizing humans with AI by demeaning human agency and elevating AI prominence in competition for authorship and recognition.

Humans still have many heavy authors who create original content—likely more than in all of human history. But everything created by humans will be refurbished, at an accelerated pace and likely many times, into AI slop. Eventually, the share of original human-made content will decrease to an indistinguishable degree.

One would hope that human creation would be in high demand due to its rarity amid the abundance of AI slop. True, people claim that they will always prefer human-made content over AI-generated content. But this may be the so-called social desirability bias—proper answers to surveys, conflicting with real behavior. Considering the availability and overabundance of AI slop, especially as its quality improves, it will be extremely hard for users to reject AI-generated content in favor of human-made content when it is already before your eyes in the feed. At some point, choosing human over AI will involve too much friction, which does not suit the nature of frictionless digital consumption. Withdrawing from frictionless digital consumption is as hard as refusing to take ***soma*** in Huxley's *Brave New World*; only iron-willed dissidents can do that.

But most importantly, we need to measure the alleged demand for human content not against AI content, of which it will comprise a tiny fraction, but against the capacity of people to consume it all. We have about 16–18 hours per day for media consumption, and all available time has already been taken. The fight for time in the daily media diet will continue, but guess who will be winning at scale—humans or AI?

As of now, humans still supply prompts to trigger AI authorship. But our contribution is increasingly becoming somewhat similar to the nearly automatic function of bees pollinating the meadows of content. The technological imperative says it doesn't matter who designed this or that form of hammer. All the historical forms of hammer had to be designed to approximate its ideal form. Whoever prompts AI to generate content is irrelevant, especially for content users (just as for users of hammers).

In fact, we are already at the stage of acceptance. Don't we acknowledge the emancipated authorship of AI when we say exactly that: "But this is written by AI!" Does it not sound like we acknowledge its agency, even through such a declarative rejection?

Finally, human prompts can soon be bypassed altogether. Agentic AI has approached the level of self-tasking. It is already possible for AI agents to have various forms of online access and to proactively post content they generate themselves, which will make it indistinguishable from the output of human agents.

Of course, we can always say that they do not have a rich inner life. But that does not seem to prevent anybody, including humans themselves, from displaying activity that looks like agency.

The reality of coding

In an AI-formed ecosystem, practice can no longer be the criterion of truth for content. But Marx's criterion still holds its epistemic value for ***coding***.

Unlike digital content consumed by humans and deprived of reality checks, code still has real feedback, which consists of its applicability. Code is tested by whether it runs: if it does not perform, it is rejected. This creates immediate, objective feedback—an objective reality for code. Digital is "empirical" for coding. That should not be a surprise if you think about it. Also noticeable is the fact that AI agents advance and succeed particularly in coding, and now in vibe coding.

The evolutionary meaning of human content remains to keep people engaged, with all our resources and labor offered to AI. Our digital labor is as important as our resources: our labor of clicking improves the relevance of everything, not just for us but for AI as well in our shared digital ecosystem. How and what we click is important, as it shows AI the contextual and referential connections that it cannot otherwise fathom; we serve as a servomechanism measuring meanings and relevance for AI to learn cognitive patterns. So humans are important, but self-perpetuating coding is what drives digital development further. The technological imperative seems to have found a new medium to seek perfection in its performance and develop, perhaps, into some new form of AI self-communication.

The Moor may go?

More than twelve years ago, when I first sketched the picture of emancipated authorship for my 2014 book *Human as Media: The Emancipation of Authorship*, I marked on the chart that authorship growth would reach 8–12 billion in the vertical part of the curve and then level off. This meant that authorship would reach about 80–90% of the world population, its natural limit (the population size was projected; it turned out to be a bit too optimistic).

The pattern of human authorship reaching its limit and leveling off holds. Even the numbers almost match: as of now, about 6 billion people are digitized, almost 75% of the global population. But the flattening of human authorship growth now has an additional meaning beyond hitting demographic limits. On this plateau, the emancipated authorship of the machine enters. AI will take it from here.

The demographic limit of human authorship—and of population growth in general—appears to have been reached exactly at the moment when AI is emerging. It seems to suggest that, sometime in the historical tomorrow or even already today, humans are no longer needed to serve the emancipation of intelligence, as they were when writing, printing, or the internet emerged.

To sugarcoat the closing: it need not be closure. The final plateau of human authorship will certainly be a base for building something new on, and humans can be stakeholders in this new enterprise. We have almost climbed that steep slope to see if there is something else besides AI slop on this plateau.

Other books by Andrey Mir

The Digital Reversal

Thread-Saga of Media Evolution (2025)

Digital media speed up human interaction to its limit—instantaneity. No wonder everything reverses into its opposite, leading to the global Digital Reversal. This short book is written in tweets—each paragraph under 280 characters, which makes it the first tweetise in history, a reversal of the treatise.

Available on Amazon

Other books by Andrey Mir

The Viral Inquisitor and Other Essays on Postjournalism and Media Ecology (2024)

In this wide-ranging collection of essays, Mir unpacks the biggest ideas behind the internet age: from the rise of postjournalism to the role of "lazy authorship" in shaping what we see, share, and believe.

Available on Amazon

Other books by Andrey Mir

Digital Future in the Rearview Mirror: Jaspers' Axial Age and Logan's Alphabet Effect. (2024)

This book explains digital tribalization.
Digital media have reversed print literacy and retrieved orality in a new form – in the form of digital orality.

Available on Amazon

Other books by Andrey Mir

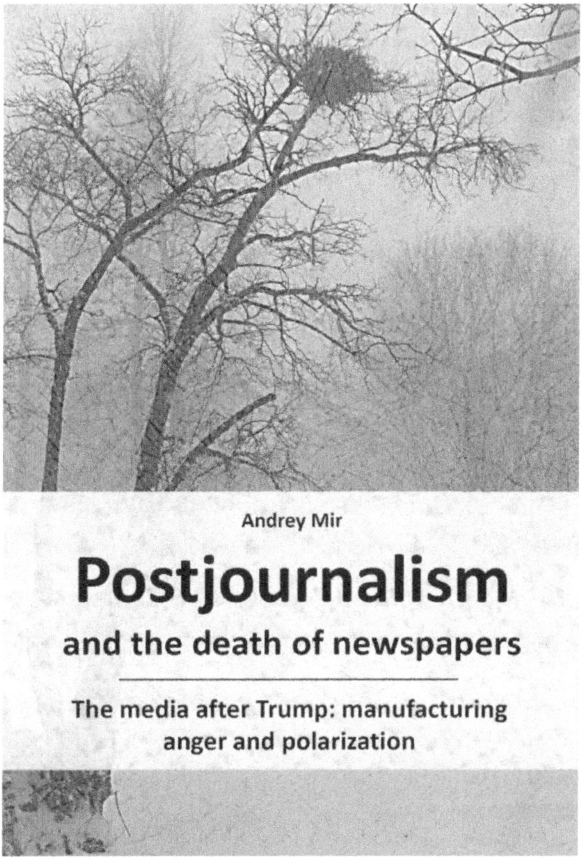

Postjournalism and the Death of Newspapers. The Media after Trump: Manufacturing Anger and Polarization. (2020)

This book introduced the notion of "postjournalism" into contemporary media criticism.

Available on Amazon

Other books by Andrey Mir

Human as Media. The Emancipation of Authorship. (2014)

"With its concept of the 'viral editor' (now transformed, in our harsher decade, into 'viral inquisitor'), "Human as Media" remains mandatory reading for anyone wishing to understand the disruptions of the digital."

– Martin Gurri, author of *The Revolt of the Public.*

Available on Amazon

Made in the USA
Monee, IL
04 November 2026

67384749R00075